D1823279

THE POLICE REVOLUTION

PETER EVANS

Routledge
Taylor & Francis Group

LONDON AND NEW YORK

First published in 1974 by George Allen & Unwin Ltd.

This edition first published in 2023
by Routledge
4 Park Square, Milton Park, Abingdon, Oxon OX14 4RN

and by Routledge
605 Third Avenue, New York, NY 10158

Routledge is an imprint of the Taylor & Francis Group, an informa business

© 1974 Peter Evans

All rights reserved. No part of this book may be reprinted or reproduced or utilised in any form or by any electronic, mechanical, or other means, now known or hereafter invented, including photocopying and recording, or in any information storage or retrieval system, without permission in writing from the publishers.

Trademark notice: Product or corporate names may be trademarks or registered trademarks, and are used only for identification and explanation without intent to infringe.

British Library Cataloguing in Publication Data
A catalogue record for this book is available from the British Library

ISBN: 978-1-032-41114-9 (Set)
ISBN: 978-1-032-45106-0 (Volume 4) (hbk)
ISBN: 978-1-032-45311-8 (Volume 4) (pbk)
ISBN: 978-1-003-37636-1 (Volume 4) (ebk)

DOI: 10.4324/9781003376361

Publisher's Note
The publisher has gone to great lengths to ensure the quality of this reprint but points out that some imperfections in the original copies may be apparent.

Disclaimer
The publisher has made every effort to trace copyright holders and would welcome correspondence from those they have been unable to trace.

THE POLICE
REVOLUTION

Peter Evans

London   George Allen & Unwin Ltd
Ruskin House   Museum Street

First published in 1974

This book is copyright under the Berne Convention. All
rights are reserved. Apart from any fair dealing for
the purpose of private study, research, criticism or review,
as permitted under the Copyright Act, 1957, no part of
this publication may be reproduced, stored in a retrieval
system, or transmitted, in any form or by any means,
electronic, electrical, chemical, mechanical, optical,
photocopying, recording or otherwise, without the prior
permission of the copyright owner. Enquiries should
be addressed to the publishers.

© Peter Evans 1974

ISBN 0 04 350048 x

To Frank Williamson

Printed in Great Britain
in 11 point Baskerville type
by William Clowes & Sons, Limited
London, Beccles and Colchester

Contents

Acknowledgements

The number of people who have given me advice or material for this book is too large for me to mention all of them individually. But my special thanks go to Mr Howard Perry, deputy editor of *Police Review*, Mr Anthony Judge, editor of *Police*, and other officials of the Police Federation, Chief Superintendent Brian Rowland, secretary of the Police Superintendents' Association, Mr John Alderson, formerly Commandant of the Police College and now Chief Constable of Devon and Cornwall, Mr G. W. R. Terry, formerly Chief Constable of Lincolnshire and now of Sussex, and Mr David Gray, Her Majesty's Chief Inspector for Constabulary for Scotland, as well as various police officers in different parts of Britain kind enough to talk frankly to me, but mention of whose names might cause them some embarrassment. Mr G. D. Gregory of Scotland Yard arranged interviews with senior officers there in connection with the role of the police and visits to see particular departments in operation. For permission to do this I thank Sir Robert Mark, the Metropolitan Police Commissioner. (I should add that my sources for background information about the leadership question at the Yard were not obtained through official channels.) I am grateful to Professor Michael Banton, whose work I have always admired, for allowing me to attend a seminar at Bristol University which was invaluable in providing a further insight into the sociology of the police. My thanks also go to civil servants at the Home Office for providing me with facts and visits to laboratories.

This book, which attempts in part to understand some of the reasons for friction between some sections of the police and of the immigrant community, would not have been possible without the frankness with which ordinary people have expressed their views. Discussions with certain M.P.s, community relations officers and immigrant leaders have also been of immense value.

I would like to pay personal tribute to Mr William Hart, who, when I knew him first, before his retirement, was Superintendent in charge of the area where I first went into journalism twenty-five years ago. He was kind enough to give a young reporter some understanding of the police, which has been of service ever since

None of the above should be held responsible for the views expressed in this book, which are, of course, personal. Indeed, some may disagree with them and with my interpretation of events. I hope that their views continue to add to discussion about the police service.

Lastly, my thanks are due to William Rees-Mogg, Editor of *The Times*, for allowing me to write this book and thus to develop knowledge I have acquired in covering the police for the newspaper.

Peter Evans
January 1974

Preface

The police have problems. If they did not there would be no need for a police force. The police force was brought into being in the nineteenth century to deal with crime and public turbulence. Today those problems have developed dangerously. Violence has increased in protest and crime, and crime has become much more sophisticated. Some politicians, worried, too, about the extent of protest by sections of the public and of inflation, fear lest democracy, as it has been known in this country, will be unable to cope and could be superseded by a more authoritarian form of government. The more extreme of the protesters feel that government in Britain is already authoritarian, and that the police are an arm of the state. It therefore seemed sensible to begin this book with a look at some of the more pressing *external* problems facing the police.

No Force has been facing greater difficulties than the Metropolitan. In many respects similar difficulties are faced by other Forces, but in London they are heightened. This is because London remains the capital of crime, it contains more targets for protest than anywhere else, including foreign embassies, and because social problems are great. For these reasons, and because no fewer than a fifth of the country's 100,000 police officers are in the Metropolitan Force, this book will give attention to it in particular, while exploring other difficulties and developments as they occur elsewhere. For example, the Scottish police have something to offer their English colleagues in their evolution of the role of the police.

Internally, too, the police face problems, and again they are nowhere more pressing than in the Metropolitan Force. It is suffering from a crippling shortage of men, and the effects of this are felt throughout the Force. This especially weakens the role of the police in the prevention of crime. Recently the Metropolitan Police, in particular, have faced allegations that their standards of conduct have slipped. In the early 1960s studies of the police reflected similar accusations against certain provincial forces, but the emphasis has since shifted.

Those who see the police as a repressive force are matched at the other extreme by others wishing for more 'law and order'. They see the police as a means of enforcing that demand.

Friction between black people and the police has caused much concern. Discussion of the relationships between them has often produced more heat than light, and it is the heat that has therefore attracted attention. It seems, in fact, more constructive to compare the natures of the two groups – blacks and police – and to examine the pressures at work on each from within and without. The result of this kind of investigation is that one discovers greater similarities between them than either has so far understood. The lessons which each has to learn from the other could, perhaps, help to reduce this friction and contribute towards a better understanding of the role of the police in society. The presence of black people serves here, as in other ways, to highlight problems that exist to some extent already.

There is pressure from two sources upon the police to change. It comes firstly from society itself, though the police would argue that it would be unwise to mistake the strength with which such opinions are expressed for the extent to which they are held. Secondly, that pressure comes from the methods which the police are adopting to enforce the law. Those pressures also raise questions about their role and how they are adapting to new techniques, particularly the increasing use of science and technology, which, some policemen believe, threatens the traditional methods of policing. The police are in a position rather similar to that of other manpower intensive industries developed in Victorian times, such as coal or the docks, whose communities have faced, and are facing, a technological revolution. There is also a 'police revolution'. But there are important differences.

From them springs the question: how far should the police resist some of the pressures upon them, to maintain the state of steady, reassuring equilibrium that would most please the public and enhance confidence within the service?

In the light of the problems facing the police, the nature of the police and the changes that are facing them, a concluding chapter will discuss some of the measures that could be taken.

I
THE POLICE AND
THEIR PROBLEMS

1 Crime

*The objects of the police cannot be fully realised – the
public's changing attitudes towards the law – the split
personality of the police – the distorted figures of crime –
violence and armed robbery – crime as a multi-national
enterprise – the 'Chinese connection' – 'hot' money
invested in business.*

'It should be understood at the outset that the principal
object to be obtained is the prevention of crime. To this
great end every effort of the Police is to be directed. The
security of person and property, the preservation of public
tranquillity, and all other objects of a Police establishment
will thus be better effected than by the detection and
punishment of the offender after he has succeeded in committing the crime. This should constantly be kept in mind
by every member of the Police Force, as a guide for his
own conduct. Officers and Police Constables should en-
deavour to distinguish themselves by such vigilance and
activity as may render it extremely difficult for anyone to
commit a crime within that portion of the town under
their charge.'

This description of the primary object of the police, laid
down by Sir Richard Mayne, the first Metropolitan Police
Commissioner, reflects the optimism with which policing
began. It is still quoted like a sacred text by police officers
striving after the original ideal. In his booklet *Thieves on
Wheels*, Deputy Assistant Commissioner David Powis refers to it in explaining why a few men in every police
division 'seem uncannily successful in arresting criminals
in the street'. He says that a car with its engine running
while stationary should always be investigated. Men, or
women for that matter, in motor-cars can 'frequent or
loiter with intent' just as they can on foot. There may be

evidence in the car justifying a subsequent prosecution for conspiring to commit a crime. Mr Powis says: 'To prevent a serious crime by such an arrest is more praiseworthy than subsequent costly detection, and is precisely within the terms of Sir Richard Mayne's *Primary Object of Police.*'

In 1973, for the first time in 20 years, crime fell by a marginal 0·7 per cent, thus raising hopes that Sir Richard's ideal might have come a fraction nearer realisation, even if violent offences did rise by a shocking 17·6 per cent. Sadly, however, there were indications at the end of the year that the previous sustained increase in recorded crime was likely to be resumed.

Most policemen realise it is illusory to think that Sir Richard's ideal can ever be completely realised. They know that, by themselves, they cannot contain crime. A lot depends upon the attitudes of the public towards the law and the way the courts work. Still more depends on the resources made available to the police and the nature of society which spawns criminals.

Mr John Alderson, formerly Commandant of the Police College, Bramshill, and now Chief Constable of Devon and Cornwall, says that, due to the shortage of policemen (particularly in the Metropolitan Force) the original preventive role of the police has been whittled away. Others, harking back to a less permissive age, would like courts to impose severe sentences as a stronger deterrent. Many, if not most, policemen would like to see murderers, particularly of policemen, hanged. These policemen think nostalgically of the uncomplicated Victorian code of ethics (in which, moreover, there was a criminal class, and wrongdoers were more easily spotted). Good and evil were more clearly defined. The law stated just what constituted crime and was based on the Christian ethic, in which most believed.

It was the belief of many Victorian penal reformers that poverty, and the hopelessness that it engendered, created crime; if the social conditions could only be improved then the need for the poor to steal would be reduced. Murder for gain, for example, would not be necessary. But the experience of Europe between 1955 and 1964 showed once and for all that crime would increase along with affluence. France saw a rise of 70 per cent in crimes per 100,000 of population; in affluent Sweden, the rise was 44 per cent, in the Netherlands 54 per cent, in Denmark 27 per cent, in Germany 26 per cent, in Austria 25 per cent, and in Italy 40 per cent.[*]

The criminal 'class' is no longer so easily identifiable, if it can be called a class at all. This is confusing for the police. Today some of the most successful criminals dress smartly and may live in a style more akin to the respectable middle classes. The police, however, depend much upon stereotypes. Young constables are taught how to recognise the sorts of people who may be up to no good from their appearance. 'Watch for', says Mr Powis, 'groups of young men dressed in "scooter type" clothing, e.g. green anoraks or "combat jackets" with the usual badges and ornamentation, who are on foot or travelling by public transport. Young motor thieves dress like this when on foot so they will not look out of place on a stolen scooter. The unusual absence of young women of a similar class from such groups of males may indicate an intention to steal.'

Obviously, the policeman, if he is to prevent crime, as Sir Richard Mayne wished, must know where to start looking and who is likely to commit it, and he will value Mr Powis's guide in this respect.

The trouble is, though, that today, with a lot of people wearing casual dress and long hair, the signals which may indicate to the policeman that a man is suspicious may be misleading. Indeed, Mr Powis recognises this when advising how to question someone who has been stopped.

---

[*] Sir Leon Radzinowicz, then Wolfson Professor of Criminology and Director of the Institute of Criminology at Cambridge University, in a lecture to *The New Bridge* on 26 April 1972.

He writes: 'The counter to the old familiar "Do I look like a criminal, officer?" is: "These days, as you see from newspapers and courts, mere appearance counts for little or nothing." The original question should be put again in a pleasant manner.'

The difficulties that the policeman is in, nevertheless, are indicated by Mr Powis's advice elsewhere in his booklet to policemen to try and observe in court persons in custody for theft or unlawful taking of motor vehicles, to 'see to which category they belong. This will help you to slant your mind to the general type of person you must watch for when patrolling.'

The effects of this difficulty sometimes recoil on the police. One very senior police officer confesses that his son was stopped one night as a suspicious person, because he was young, casually dressed and had long hair. Another man stopped was an assistant prison governor who had decided to walk through some side streets and, being keenly interested in cars, was looking at them as he passed. Two policemen questioned him and, when he gave an explanation, one said: 'I wonder what your prisoners will think when they hear about you being in the nick.' After an unpleasant few minutes they allowed him to go.

The greatest difficulty comes in dealing with the young black population in places like Handsworth (Birmingham), Brixton or Notting Hill. The police believe that in Brixton black youths are responsible for much, if not most, of the mugging cases there. That being their opinion, they therefore look out for groups of black youngsters behaving suspiciously. In Brixton, in a recreation hall run by a multi-racial organisation called 'The Melting Pot', fifteen black youths said they had all been in trouble of some sort with the police, though none admitted to mugging anyone. They said that, even if they were doing nothing and intending to do nothing, they were in constant danger of being stopped by the police and maybe arrested as suspected persons loitering with intent – 'on "sus" ' as they call it. They clearly felt that the reason why they were stopped was simply because they were black. In other words, they were being categorised by their appearance rather as were, in other circumstances, young people wearing anoraks with the usual badges on them.*

So what are the police to do? One of their most useful powers, from the point of view of crime prevention, is to stop and search, though this is in theory confined to certain places, London amongst them. (The police have wider powers to search for firearms and drugs, and stopping young people to look for the latter has led to ill-feeling.) Loitering with intent is an old offence (Sections 4 and 6 of the Vagrancy Act, 1824, as amended). It covers 'every suspected person or reputed thief frequenting or loitering about or in any river, canal, or navigable stream, dock, or basin, or any quay, wharf, or warehouse near or adjoining thereto, or any street, highway, or avenue leading thereto, or any street or highway, or any place adjacent to a street or highway, with intent to commit an arrestable offence'.

Against this, of course, the police officer has another power – of discretion. But in the face of the immense amount of crime, particularly of violence and petty thieving, the police are under tremendous pressure to keep the streets safe for people to walk on.

Trying sensitively to keep in step with modern opinion gives cause for police frustration. Although great attempts are made to create a common policy for dealing with offences, the police are made up of individual human beings, each with some power of discretion. If the police display too liberal an attitude they may find themselves criticised by hard-line members of the public. Hard-line policies, on

* Mr F. H. McClintock, then acting director of the Institute of Criminology, Cambridge, told a Council of Europe conference in 1972 that the number of immigrants (from Ireland and the Commonwealth) involved in crimes of violence rose more steeply between 1950 and 1960 than did the number of indigenous people involved in such crimes, and accounted for 70 per cent of the total increase in the number of adult offenders.

the other hand, may get them into trouble with the liberals. In enforcing the law against pornography, for instance, the police are caught between the Scylla of the Festival of Light, an organisation which wants to raise the moral standards of the nation, and the Charybdis of the free-thinking liberals.

Sir Robert Mark, the Metropolitan Police Commissioner, tried to produce a rationale for the relationship between the police and public over the enforcement of the law in his Edwin Stevens Lecture, *The Disease of Crime – Punishment or Treatment*, given on 20 June 1972 at the Royal Society of Medicine. 'A force of just over 100,000 men serving a population of over 50 million, one police officer to 500 citizens, must clearly be sensitive to the reactions of both courts and people. Such a situation compels discretion in enforcement policies and the use of resources.'

People would generally help the police to combat crimes that offended their own sense of morality, such as murder or sexual offences involving violence, he said. They were largely indifferent to crimes about which they did not feel strongly, and in which their own interests did not suffer, such as fraud, shoplifting, and cheating the excise or revenue authorities. They were sometimes hostile to the enforcement of laws that affected them personally.

Crime meant different things to different people, he added. It differed from country to country as well as from decade to decade. Bigamy, once a felony in Great Britain subject to heavy penalties, was now unlikely to lead to prosecution unless it involved fraud or seduction by misrepresentation. The attitude of legislators to abortion, off-course betting and homosexuality had undergone extensive change in the past few years.

Some policemen feel that they can never win. In dealing with the black population, for instance, their dilemma is particularly acute. At a conference on race relations held in 1972 at the Commonwealth Institute, an example of initiative by the Police Federation, genuinely puzzled policemen asked the team of experts on race whether they should enforce the law against black people holding noisy parties late at night where drinks may be sold, they said, without licence. The experts said they should. The police replied that this led to complaints of harassment against them.

Recent changes in attitudes towards the offender also put police in a dilemma. Part of their technique in dealing with crime is to look out for likely suspects, as we have seen. Another is the belief that a real leopard does not change its spots. That is why they keep files of finger-prints, pictures of known criminals, and devote dossiers to them and their habits. Penal reformers think that, if the aim is to cure crime, such police methods frequently do not help. One of the modern theories of criminology concerns 'labelling'. In other words, if a dog is given a bad name, he will live up to it. Penal reformers, and offenders themselves, believe that, once a debt to society has been paid, they should be free to make a fresh start. This belief in the innate goodness of people and the possibility of reforming them is diametrically opposed to the beliefs of the more cynical. To paraphrase Voltaire: Suppose that you could sit by the fire in Paris, a glass of brandy at your elbow, and, by pressing a button, you could end the life of your rich old aunt in Cairo, who had left you all her money – how many of you would not press the button?

Another way of putting the question these days is: How many of you would be willing to fiddle expenses, or to put private letters in the office mail, or to use the office telephone to make private calls? Criminologists call this white-collar crime, and compare leniency towards the people who commit it with the more severe treatment of overalled workers who pilfer the odd small piece of equipment from a factory: some say that this reflects a lingering class attitude in the police towards crime. An inquiry by the British Security Industry Association reported in 1973 that losses through pilfering (or what may just be regarded as the perks of the job) amounted to about £12 million a year. Items that go missing range from pens, paperclips, and pencils, to typewriters, calculators, tape-recorders and Pirelli calendars. A sample of large office-blocks in London revealed that on average each year they lost more than one per cent of their supplies and equipment because of pilfering.

Many policemen are puzzled by what they regard as a soft attitude towards offenders, and their difficulties are not dispelled by government policy that decrees that while practised, professional criminals who are a real menace to society, particularly if they are dangerous, should be sent to prison for stiff sentences, the less dangerous should serve their sentences in the community.

For the conscientious policeman, doing his best to reflect the attitudes of society and the courts, there appear to be contradictions. How is he to regard baby-bashing, for example? Should it be treated as a crime to be punished severely or as a symptom of something wrong with the parents that has to be cured rather than punished? Will dragging parents through the courts stop it?

The statistics are alarming. Dr Gerard Vaughan M.P., Consultant Physician at Guy's Hospital, told a conference organised by the Royal Institute of Public Health and Hygiene, on 21 November 1972, that about six in every 1,000 live children born would be beaten up. Of 500,000 new births each year, probably 3,000 children would be battered, and the number was going up. The child would probably first be bruised, usually about the head or face, and taken to a general practitioner, who would find little or nothing wrong, and fail to recognise the parents' cry for help, as Dr Vaughan put it. The child would then be more severely beaten, and again the G.P. would be likely to think little of it. At least 60 per cent of those children would be severely beaten, 15 per cent – several hundred a year – would have permanent brain damage, and 10 per cent would die. Ninety per cent of those dead children would have had one or two major injuries before death, and one or several visits to doctors without the true condition being realised. And, at the time, 52 per cent of the mothers would be pregnant again.

Most policemen, like most prisoners, believe that there is nothing worse than offences against children. Sometimes men in prison, who have committed sexual offences against them, with an element of violence, ask to be put into solitary confinement to escape the wrath of their fellow-prisoners. Of course, baby-bashing is not in quite the same category, though it is likely to cause deep revulsion. Nevertheless, some sections of the police are beginning to look at the social causes of such offences. How far the police should fulfil a social role like this causes fierce debate within the service.

The debate about whether police should have a social role is really part of a wider discussion about how best to deploy resources. Too little is known still about the extent of crime for the police to gauge with any precision what effect they are having on it.

The police keep statistics, but increasingly they and students of criminology are aware how artificial they are. Not all crime is reported, for a start, so it never ends up in the figures. Sir Leon Radzinowicz said in his lecture to *The New Bridge* on 26 April 1972 that there were two main figures of concealment – the hidden figure of crimes – offences which never come to the notice of the police, and the hidden figure of criminals, which covers, in addition, those whose offences are known to the police but are never brought home to their perpetrators.

'In England and Wales, for example, only about 300,000 people a year are found guilty of indictable offences, though $1\frac{1}{2}$ million such offences are recorded. No European country gets to the bottom of more than half its recorded crimes: only Germany and Austria claim even that. In England, France, Sweden, the Netherlands, six in ten crimes go unsolved, in Denmark and Italy more than seven, in the United States eight. And the highest rates of impunity are enjoyed by the robbers and the burglars, above all by the professional criminals who plan their escapes as methodically as they plan their crimes.'

He added:

'We cannot escape the conclusion that beneath the published figures lurks a far larger bulk of crime and criminals. This dark figure of crime includes the offences committed by people of the utmost respectability. Even the maxim that murder will out is questionable. There have been too many examples of murderers who have got away with a whole string of killings without arousing suspicion before being brought to justice. There have been too many cases of deaths originally attributed to accident or suicide, but subsequently discovered to be murders. And if murder can be hidden, so can almost any other crime.'

Sir Leon suggested that those shadowy figures might multiply those for known offences by two, three, by five or even more. So, not only are police frustrated by the knowledge that they can never prevent more than a fraction of crime, they know that a lot of it cannot be detected. Worse, they do not even know that it has taken place.

This is well illustrated by what happened after the police opened a permanent station in the Blackhill district of Glasgow. In 1971 only three breach of the peace cases were dealt with by police. But in just under a year after the station was opened, in April 1972, there were seventy-four breach of the peace cases. Only one case of common assault was reported in 1971 and two cases of wife assault. After the opening of the police station there were, in just under a year, fifteen cases of common assault and twenty-one of wife assault. The figures do not, of course, mean that there has been more trouble, only that the police know of it.

This raises an important question. Could the converse

also be true? If the presence of the police uncovers more crime, will not the inability of the police to maintain as close a contact with the community as both would like mean that fewer offences are known to them? Some policemen believe this to be happening. So part of any improvement in the official figures could be not because less crime is being committed, but because it is never officially reported. This implies that official figures of this kind should be treated with caution.

On the other hand, the methods used by police to record crime may exaggerate certain other trends. Mr Stanley Klein, a Home Office official, writing in *Social Trends No. 3, 1972*, said that figures for violent crime might reflect police attitudes and the varying ways of recording offences rather than any real increase. It was disturbing, he said, that indictable offences known to the police in 1971 were two and a half times the figure in 1961. But that had to be seen in the context of crime as a whole.

'Over 95 per cent of crimes known', he said, 'are offences against property. Offences of violence against the person fluctuate between two per cent and three per cent of the total; these and sexual offences are never more than five per cent of all recorded crime.'

Mr Klein said that any statistics about offences known to the police had to be treated cautiously because of the lack of uniformity in recording them. He said: 'At present, cases which are treated as non-indictable assault in some police forces are dealt with as indictable offences in other forces and there is evidence to suggest that the tendency to record minor offences as indictable has been increasing for some time.' Recent statistics showed a decrease of non-indictable assaults, by 13.4 per cent, between 1961 and 1971. This contrasted with the rapidly rising figures of indictable offences. Mr Klein added: 'It could be that offences have become more serious but it seems more probable that the police have become more inclined to treat assaults as indictable offences of wounding.'

There are two points to add to Mr Klein's comment.

The first is that police forces in Britain, as far as is compatible with overall efficiency, like to retain their own ways of doing things – a reflection of their claims to be independent, so far as operations are concerned, from the Home Office. Indeed, some criminologists would claim that statistics may sometimes be used by the police to make a case for more resources. Establishments are 'bogus' in any case, and the best result that can be got out of a bargaining process – not necessarily a true reflection of current needs. The second point is that cases which the police can quote as now commonplace do point to an increase in viciousness of the attacks on people, with the new feature of old people being singled out as targets.

On 9 August 1972 Mr Robert Carr, Home Secretary, said in a written Parliamentary answer that he accepted in principle the main recommendations of the Departmental Committee on Criminal Statistics. He hoped to make a start on putting them into effect, beginning with statistics of crimes of violence against the person, when resources were available. Although the statistics contained a lot of information about court proceedings, they provided relatively little about offences known to the police. For example, they did not analyse crimes of violence according to the degree of injury or the circumstances, such as whether they were domestic brawls, fights between adolescents or offences associated with property offences.

This is an example of the way in which exact knowledge may be hidden away in police files, but not collated in a way which can inform debate or help guide the allocation of resources and direction of action. Nevertheless, enough *is* known to indicate the immense burden placed upon the police by crime, particularly in London.

London had more planned robbery than any other Western European city, although there was far more in New York and other places in America, Mr McClintock told the Council of Europe Conference on violence in society, in 1972. Armed robberies were also more prevalent in London than in other European cities, but firearms were not so often carried, and were seldom used in planned robberies. (Indeed, the Metropolitan Police figures for 1972 showed a slight decrease in the use of fire-arms.) The conference was told that, in London, offences of robbery against people carrying money or valuables displayed the biggest increase between 1950 and 1960 and the figure had continued to increase since. Cash and property stolen in all robberies in London rose in value from £400,000 in 1960 to £2·8 million in 1970. (In 1972 the figure reached £3 million.)

Offenders in 'mugging' cases tended to be under 21, but their victims did not all come from high income or professional classes, and many belonged to the same ethnic group, social class and neighbourhood as the offenders. On the Continent, as in Britain, juvenile offenders seemed to be involved in wilful wounding at an increasingly early age. However, cases of violence against the person not involving theft are by no means restricted to the young. A third of such crimes in the London area took place in domestic situations. A very high proportion of offenders and victims alike were over 35 years old. Most of the violence not involving theft was not for criminal purposes, nor were weapons used, though assailants often grabbed objects to hand. Only one victim in ten had to be detained in hospital overnight.

The police are in the front line against violence. Each year something like 8,000 police officers are assaulted, many of them seriously. The strength of police opinions reveals the extent of frustration. They see the bloodstained, sometimes crippled victims, and say forcibly that some of the understanding shown to criminals ought, instead, to be applied to the people they attack.

The police have increasingly become victims of attacks. A study by Chief Superintendent R. M. Stobart, while on a senior command course at the Police College, Bramshill in 1971 showed that assaults on them in one urban force increased by 66 per cent between 1966 and 1970. In another, the number of spells of sickness as a result of assault rose by 56 per cent over the same period. Mr Stobart suggested five factors that decided the number and severity of attacks on the police: the attitude of offenders to the police; the ability of officers to protect themselves in violent situations; the level of police activity; the frequency with which people drank to excess; and the frequency of violent demonstrations. Most officers were hurt when arresting violent criminals and when suppressing a disorder in which drink had played a part. The proportion of cases in which weapons were used was broadly the same in each force: about 20 per cent. No officers were injured by the discharge of firearms. 'The absence of gunshot wounds is an encouraging sign but should not be over-emphasised,' he said. 'The continuing increase in the use of firearms in violent crime is likely to lead to further tragic encounters for the police.' In general, the weapons used were those at hand and were not carried for the purpose. Motor vehicles, 'the weapon most frequently used', appeared to be highly dangerous. In every case of this kind recorded in the study, the vehicle was driven deliberately at an officer and hit him. In several cases, officers were fortunate to escape without fatal injuries.

The nature of the weapons carried by criminals has implications, of course, for the debate about whether the police should be armed. Research done by Chief Inspector Colin Greenwood, one of the leading authorities in the police on firearms, at the Institute of Criminology, Cambridge in 1970–1, supported the idea that more people were prepared to use violence in the course of stealing than ever before. He said in his book *Firearms Control* that, although the firearm was, of course, the most dangerous weapon available to the robber, more injuries were caused by other weapons. He said:

'When firearms are involved, the pattern which seems to emerge is for the minimum number (most frequently, one) to carry a gun, and for the others to be armed with coshes, pick handles or ammonia. Shooting is rare and the role of the gun is to intimidate. It is clear that much emphasis is placed on shock and on the relatively short period when all those around will be stunned into inactivity. The blunt instruments and ammonia are often used to increase the shock and to incapacitate those who are in the way at the outset. In addition to its shock-producing role, the firearm appears also to be used to prevent interference and to facilitate escape and, in most cases, it is only when the firearm is being used in this role that shots are fired at people. In its earlier role of inducing shock, the firearm is, on some occasions, fired into the air or towards the ceiling.'

The more successful the police are, the more the criminal is forced to change his methods to keep one jump ahead. This also affects his view about the use of violence and harsh sentences imposed as a deterrent. In a letter to the National Association for the Care and Resettlement of Offenders, a prisoner in Category 'A', a class for whom escape must be made extremely difficult, wrote from prison in August 1971: 'Criminals faced with the consequences of their acts – imprisonment for a long, long time – do desperate things.' Because crime was becoming increasingly difficult, he said, the nature of the offences was altering.

To prevent crime, it has long been the hope of some policemen and criminologists that Britain will develop into a cashless society. It is argued that the less cash that is carried in transit and the more cheques and credit cards that are used, the less opportunity there will be for criminals to steal it *en route*. The development of the cashless society is evolving a new breed of crooks. Fraud is a growth industry.

An example of the sophistication of one type of offence came up at the Old Bailey on 28 March 1973 when a team of three pleaded guilty to conspiring to defraud banks by false pretences. One of the team admitted to being involved in the fraud to the extent of £140,000, but the others did not admit to getting more than a few thousand pounds, said Mr Michael Wosley, prosecuting. The scheme rested on the theft of cheques, which were then cashed at £30 a time with the backing of cheque cards that were also stolen. When the men were arrested, he said, two of them told Det. Sgt. John Stevens, of Scotland Yard, that it was 'better than printing money' to travel round Britain with stolen cheques.

They laid their plans so well that one even became a patient in Guy's hospital, so that he could steal cheque books from doctors. The banks, who have their own security advisers and work closely with the police, were said by Mr Wosley to have taken steps to stop money being drawn by crooks in this fashion, by ensuring that a cheque book is stamped every time a cheque card is used.

Another example of the way that criminals are shifting their attention from cash to other paper transactions is an international racket in counterfeit airline tickets. Mr A. R. Stephens, director of security and fraud prevention with the International Air Transport Association, said on 13 April 1971 that total losses to world airlines from all fraud and theft, including tickets, could not be less than £40 million. For the first time armed raids were being made on ticket agencies. There had already been two that year in Washington. IATA's office, then in Montreal, received reports almost daily of ticket thefts from one airline or another. Figures given at a seminar held by IATA showed that preventive measures were achieving some success. In the United States in 1969, the average raid on a travel agent's office resulted in a loss of 1,000 tickets. By 1970, the figure was down to 500 and in the first three months of 1971, it had sunk further to 185. Cases were known of stolen tickets being bought at half the published price from unlikely sources, which even included barmen.

This illustrates how fashions in crime spread across frontiers, increasing the difficulties of detection and necessitating better co-ordination between police forces. This is also made necessary by the increasing mobility of criminals. The building of motorways in Britain made it possible for thieves to steal in one town and flee quickly to a hide-out many miles away. Car thieves have more recently been contributing to increasing crime between Britain and the Continent. The confidence of the thieves was such that police knew of vehicles being stolen from car parks in the commuter belt or in London in the morning and being sold in Belgium or Holland the same afternoon before the owner had returned. Thieves first watched the cars so that documents could be forged and the owner's movements checked, to ensure the theft and transit would go smoothly. There is a growing trade in expensive cars stolen on the Continent and brought into Britain for sale, often to unsuspecting buyers. International crime between Britain and the Continent is expected to become even more tempting now that Britain has joined the Common Market and cross-channel travel is becoming more routine. Already criminals are known to commute to Britain for a day's shoplifting or even house-breaking.

The fact that the world is becoming smaller through better communications has encouraged the flourishing of legitimate multinational companies. Every kind of legitimate business has its criminal counter-part, flourishing like weeds. Sometimes the fraudulent firm appears to be honest. Mr J. W. Crane, Deputy Assistant Commissioner in charge of Scotland Yard's fraud squad, said in December, 1972 that company fraud was increasing on international and more complex lines. Fraudsmen in one project could embrace two or three, and quite commonly four or five countries.

'You may have a fraud conceived in New York, with a second stage in Panama, a third in Bermuda and a fourth in Switzerland or in Britain,' he said. He gave the example of a bank established in one of the off-shore havens with an administrative office in Switzerland and an accommodation address in the City of London to give it a facade of integrity. Throughout the world business institutions looked on commercial interests in London as being the most honest of all. He added: 'You may find that part of the crime is committed in each of the countries, but in no one country is there evidence sufficient to say that they have committed an offence there, but collectively it is a fraud.'

Fraud these days presents the police with complexities not only because of the territories it can embrace, but also because of the system used to create an air of respectability. One example of this is what is called the long-firm, or long-term, fraud. Mr Colin Woods, the Yard's Assistant Commissioner in charge of the criminal investigation department, said: 'You set up a phoney business and you get goods delivered. Then you make off with them. It saves you having people on wet and windy corners.'

Mr Crane explained:

'They set up a company, open credit facilities with suppliers and order increasing amounts of goods. In the past, this might have taken only six months to operate. But the long-firm fraud job is extending the activity. The criminal may acquire a well-conducted business. He may put front men in. He may run it for three years. At the end of the period, he has built up an enormous credit. He might have sold these goods at no profit, but then comes the big kill. Enormous orders go into the firm and they are literally moved out overnight. Sums involving £80,000 or £100,000 are quite common, and even £500,000 is no exaggeration.'

Some goods went to street markets in small quantities. Larger quantities went to discount firms which were buying goods very cheaply anyway to run their business and did not necessarily know that some of them could have been stolen. Part of the increasing difficulty in identifying what was the result of fraud and what was not was the need for firms to sell off stock by reducing prices when certain lines were over-produced. Some of the firms who lost out on the fraud by seeing the goods they supplied vanish without payment had become philosophical. When they fixed prices generally, they built into them a factor to take account of expected losses by fraud.

This blurring of the distinction between goods legitimately and illegitimately obtained not only makes detection difficult but salves the conscience of shoppers. If they suspect that the goods they are buying could be stolen or the result of fraud, they can placate themselves with the belief that the goods could really be the end of a line that manufacturers are selling to clear stocks. Similarly with the discovery of an antique 'find' in a street market: without extensive inquiries, which may run sooner or later into a blank wall anyway, the buyer maintains blissful ignorance of the fact that it may really be part of the haul from a burglary.

In no field are international links so well established as in drugs. They are moved on an international scale, and in many cases via the United Kingdom. There have been instances of cannabis going from here to Canada, Australia, the United States and many other countries. A lot of LSD has gone from Britain to Scandinavia. LSD can be produced in tablets the size of a pinhead or hidden in sheets of gelatine. You need only a small quantity of LSD to get 'a trip'. Some other methods of concealment are in the knots of ties, soles of shoes, or under lapels. Obviously, to have any hope of success, police need either to have leads on which to act or sufficient manpower to conduct wide enough surveillance or searches. The trouble is that, if searches are widespread, innocent people may become indignant and the police be criticised for infringement of civil liberties.

Readers may be aware from the film *The French Connection* of the traffic in drugs between France and the United States. This was the route for the channelling of heroin from the Mediterranean. Detective Inspector M. Huins, of the Yard's drug squad, believed that the British equivalent, though on a very small scale in comparison, would be the Chinese connection. Most of the illicit heroin in this country is known as Chinese 'H', which is produced in the Far East for smoking. It arrives in the United Kingdom from Hong Kong and Singapore and most is initially distributed by Chinese.

Heroin comes from poppies grown in Turkey, Greece, Persia, Afghanistan, Pakistan and India and South East Asia, particularly Laos, Cambodia, Burma and China. The most potent poppies grow in a high dryish climate. Raw opium is harvested from the poppy. This is a brown, lumpy substance, from which opium can be prepared for smoking, as it is used by the Chinese, or chewing for medicinal purposes, as is the practice of Indians and Pakistanis. From raw opium morphine is made, and heroin from the morphine. If heroin is not kept in the right conditions, it reverts to morphine.

Crime prevention is hampered firstly by the fact that poppies grow wild in their places of origin, or are legitimately grown and harvested in some places to produce medical supplies. Clamping down on illicit growing is difficult as this often happens in areas with meagre government control. Another reason is that it is a profitable crop, which encourages illicit cultivation. Huge profits can be made on the black market.

Much of Chinese 'H' is grown in the so-called golden triangle of Laos, Cambodia and Burma, and reaches Hong Kong via Thailand and Bangkok. A lot is processed into heroin in the back streets of Hong Kong. Interpol's annual conference in October, 1970, was told that the increased movement of young people internationally helped to introduce them to drug-taking and tempted them to dabble in trafficking. What particularly worries police is the appreciable increase in most countries of drug offences committed by minors. Young people have increasingly robbed chemists' shops to obtain supplies for the black market, and this has reached alarming proportions in, for instance, New Zealand and West Germany. Thus, isolating Britain from world-wide trends is difficult for law enforcement agencies.

Drug-taking and trafficking in Britain follow trends which police try to anticipate. In the early 1960s, up to 1966–7, there were rogue doctors misusing the National Health Service and the prescription system, so that large quantities of drugs were allowed into the wrong hands. Then cannabis and LSD came into fashion, with an increase in the misuse of amphetamines. Acts passed in 1968 controlled more tightly the distribution of heroin and similar drugs. Money has been taken out of the black market in these sort of drugs because addicts are now being treated under the National Health Service. There has recently been a gradual increase in the use of illicit supplies (either by theft or by addicts disposing of part of those prescribed by them) or by the import of Chinese 'H'. It was originally intended for smoking, but contains caffeine and many impurities and is dangerous to inject, which is the way in which it is usually ingested in Britain.

Because of the wide publicity given to the dangers of heroin, some people have turned to cocaine, feeling that they are safer on it. Other people have cultivated cannabis plants privately in Britain. Scotland Yard's drug squad came across more than twenty cases in 1972 – another example of the way that offenders adapt new techniques to try and keep ahead of police methods.

There might seem to be some satisfaction for policemen, trying to follow Sir Richard Mayne's original intention of preventing crime, in the signs revealed in 1971 that addiction to heroin and perhaps some other dangerous drugs was not increasing at the rate forecast. Indeed, Americans feel that they have something to learn from British methods generally in dealing with the problem. But there have been some increases in other forms of drug abuse.

After the law was changed to restrict heroin and supplies dried up, addicts turned to the injection of barbiturates, the sedatives that are in common use in Britain. There are over 15 million National Health Service prescriptions for barbiturates a year, and any amount of private ones as well. Abrupt withdrawal of barbiturates from someone who has been taking them to excess may have an alarming and sometimes fatal consequence. Though the average mortality rate of 8 per cent is relatively low, barbiturates cause more deaths than any other solid or liquid poison in the United States.

Thus drugs, like other new and developing forms of crime, provide opportunities for international law-breaking on a gigantic scale. While drugs and fraud present major and complex forms of law enforcement, police in Britain have been successful in preventing so far the sort of organised crime that has flourished in the United States, though our entry into the Common Market is bound to strengthen links between criminals here and on the Continent.

So far the picture in Britain has been very different from that in the United States. There the Cosa Nostra confederation is one of America's largest business enterprises, according to Professor Donald Cressey, a special consultant on the United States Presidential Commission on law enforcement and administration of justice in 1966–7. The Commission estimated that confederated crime cost Americans about 9,000 million dollars a year, more than all other types of crime combined and about double the amount spent annually in the United States for all police, court and correctional work.

The Americans had financial interests, investments and influence in Britain, just as they did in other European countries, Professor Cressey said. Confederated crime was not now prevalent in Britain. But only five years before, participants in the American confederation offered technical assistance to under-developed British criminals and others. 'Britain narrowly escaped,' he said. 'Had the involved British criminals known as much about business methods as they knew about extortion; had the FBI and Scotland Yard been less diligent; and had the gambling laws not been changed, the Americans could well have established outposts here, as they have established them in Canada and the Bahamas.' He conceded that Britain did not seem ripe either for the development of a domestic confederation of criminals or an American take-over. But he added: 'Sooner or later, criminals learn that the safest crimes are those involving fraud rather than violence or stealing, and British criminals are beginning to catch on.'

Considering the sums that it is possible to obtain through fraud and other crime, it is inevitable, too, that British criminals will obtain knowledge about how to invest their proceeds. These are large. The annual survey of theft losses carried out by *Security Gazette*, and published in October, 1972, showed that police forces recorded about £74 million in money and property stolen in the United Kingdom in 1971. Only about £14 million was recovered, leaving the thieves with a tax-free profit of £60 million from crimes known to the police. But, said the article, these recorded figures are 'generally regarded as representing only the "tip of the iceberg" in relation to the great volume of stealing which must go on, unsuspected or unreported, throughout the country.'

Buying valuable stamps is one obvious outlet, partly because they are so easy to conceal. The money is also invested in legitimate businesses, and senior police officers have been worrying about the implications. The short step to the establishment of companies in which to invest funds is known already to have been taken in some cases, but so far in only a minor way. Once this practice becomes the rule, the line between legitimate and illegitimate business is further blurred as a result of crime. And when this happens, proper managerial expertise will be employed in crime to match the skill in planning and the daring in execution that are already being displayed. Scotland Yard already know of managerial skills being bought to aid investment of the proceeds of crime, but not so far in a big way. Once they are, organised crime could become established in Britain, with links to the Continent,

America, indeed even on a world-wide scale. To prevent this developing from its present embryonic growth is a major police strategy.

Thus it can be seen how difficult the task of the police has become in terms of trying to fulfil their original objectives. The changing pattern of crime, the inadequacy of statistics that could provide more knowledge, and the sophistication of the modern criminal operating across frontiers in a way that governments and police forces have yet to match, all conspire against attainment of those objectives. This does not mean that their objectives do not constitute the noble expression of an ideal, but in truth they are beyond the capacity of the police to attain by themselves, and this should be realised, particularly by government. Meanwhile, on other fronts, changes have also taken place which have led to self-doubts among the police about their ability to fulfil their role.

2 The Police and the Public

Peaceful protest becomes violent – the politicians and the police – the gap between police and public – nineteenth-century fears echo today – the public's opinion of the police.

As protest in recent years has become more widespread and shrill, policemen have been hard-pressed on some occasions to maintain public tranquillity. The fact is that they had no more chance of doing that by themselves than of removing the causes of crime. The causes of crime and public turbulence lie elsewhere. All the police have been able to do is control public turbulence when it breaks the surface, or is about to do so.

When public turbulence does break the surface the British policeman on the whole behaves extraordinarily well. He has, with some noteworthy exceptions, become adept at handling protests and demonstrations, though this was not always so. Recent expertise has been built up since the 1960s. Demonstrations in this era began with protests by the Campaign for Nuclear Disarmament, and were essentially non-violent. The police had a comparatively easy job, shepherding the procession of marchers into and through London, keeping traffic moving, and eventually controlling unobtrusively the vast crowds in Trafalgar Square and giving people the chance to let their views be heard.

Occasionally, as in the case of an anti-apartheid demonstration in 1960, there was violence, but not anti-police violence. Trouble started when the demonstration broke up and fighting broke out between some of the demonstrators and waiting right-wing extremists. The incident made big news at the time.

Demonstrating against apartheid was a reaction to events abroad over which the British people had no direct control. The surge of protests against the Vietnam war was also a reaction to news from overseas. In Britain, at least, these sorts of protest were a natural reflection of two developments – the weakening of British power abroad, which no longer enabled the government to exercise decisive influence on world events, and the improvement in communications, which brought, for example, atrocities in Vietnam to the world's television screens, thus rousing the emotions of people who were unable to do very much about them, except to protest publicly.

These public emotions, once they are channelled into public protest, provide ideal raw material for extremists to manipulate. The 1968 protest against Vietnam was an example. For holders of extreme views Vietnam was part of a world pattern in which America, a neo-Fascist state, was leading the exploitation of Third World countries. To these extremists the conflict was between repressive capitalism and the poor working class. Their task at demonstrations was to make it seem that that was what the protest was about, whereas, in fact, there is always a multiplicity of motives among those taking part on such occasions. Many people were sickened at the conduct of the war, with the use of defoliants and body counts. Others were simply against the war as such.

One agitator told me how it was he, in one of the anti-Vietnam demonstrations, who led the marchers away from Downing Street towards Grosvenor Square. His particular technique was to sit on the ground, once the objective was in sight, and let the marchers continue on their way round him, until he was able to get up and make his escape. To such extremists the British police are not wonderful. They set out in the first place to provoke the police, carry marbles to scatter under police horses and hat-pins to stick into them. Police at demonstrations are used to wiping spittle from their faces, and some of them nurse injuries afterwards. There is nothing these extremists would like better than a running battle with the police, so that pictures of angry British bobbies punching demonstrators, and thus seen as brutally quelling legitimate protest, would be wired round the world.

Since the election of the Conservative Government in 1970, and the withdrawal of America from Vietnam, protests by the native British have become once more largely about domestic issues and, although their size has tended to decrease, they make up for that in their number and vehemence. Of course, there are still a number of protests against events abroad, such as those over the Pakistan-India war, or the treatment of Jews in Russia, or the clash between Israel and the Arabs. Some police divisions are kept extraordinarily busy. Within Britain, some of the angriest of more recent protests have been of trade unionists against the Conservative government's Industrial Relations Bill, which protesters saw as interference with basic trade union rights. It was of little consequence to the demonstrators that the government was elected with a mandate from the people to do its job.

Increasingly protest comes also from disaffected minorities, whether over anti-inflation measures, the building of a motorway destroying the environment of a section of the public, or the proposed siting of a third London airport. This again places the police in an invidious position. If the third London airport had been built at Cublington, and local people had resisted removal, as they said they would, whose side would the friendly local bobby have been on? The position is potentially difficult over the enforcement of some laws in Wales. For instance, concern has been expressed in high quarters about the alleged leniency of the sentences imposed by some magistrates on Welsh language demonstrators.

Thus it can be seen that the police can do little about the real causes of public turbulence. This is a reflection of the gap between government and people, which senior politicians are increasingly worried about. Some believe that, with the centre of economic decision-taking in Brussels now that Britain has joined the Common Market, ordinary people will be even less able to influence the decisions that affect them. Martin Luther King once said that riots are the voice of the unheard, and the relevance of that remark applies more widely than just to the black minority. There seems to be a new political law at work: the larger the unit, the harder it is to please all the people within it all the time, when decisions are taken for the greater good of the greater number. The policeman, whose job is supposed to be essentially non-political, is caught in the middle, trying to maintain public tranquillity, as the gap between government and sections of the public widens. The police are fully aware of the difficulties of their task, and the thinking behind briefings of policemen before demonstrations is conscious of the need for restraint, and this is sustained by discipline training.

More recently, violence has added to the difficulties of the policing of protest. Letter-bombs through the post, bomb attacks in city streets, the attempted assassination of a foreign diplomat, the occupation of an embassy, and instances such as the entry gained by a group of Pakistanis to the Indian High Commission – all make acute demands upon the judgement and diligence of the police.

This swelling tide of protest is at one extreme of the relationship between police and public. The other is in the more subtle interplay of pressures, checks and balances, in day-to-day contacts at local level. Much depends upon understandings built up over the years, through the process of give and take. The police and public are conscious of what each expects of the other, and this is more apparent in rural areas, where contact is closer and more personal. Even the mundane can become important.

The point was well illustrated in a Gloucestershire village. For forty years a halt-sign had been ignored by a now elderly cyclist on his twice-daily ride to work. He came down the hill just fast enough to carry him up the slight incline over the halt-sign and thus on to the level of the main road running along the valley, in this way saving his old bones. One day a policeman, new in the village and anxious to exert authority, shouted at him to stop. He was so shocked he fell off his bicycle and broke his spectacles. The result of this quite trivial incident was that, because the man was a regular customer of a public house at the centre of village life, the policeman aroused resentment, lost the support of the village and found it more difficult to do his job.

Sometimes a village may exert sanctions against the policeman and his family. Anthony Judge in *A Man Apart* tells how a village shop-keeper banned a policeman's wife from his premises because her husband had reported him for a motoring offence. She had to go several miles to the nearest town for her groceries. Maureen Cain relates in *Society and the Policeman's Role* that she was told by an officer in one county force: 'There's a certain barrier between you and the other members of the public, and if you break it awkward situations can arise.' Another said: 'You make a barrier for yourself. In the country it's essential.' Other communities exert different pressures. Mr Dan Wilson of the Scottish Police Federation said at a Police Federation Seminar in June 1971: 'Only recently, we had to take legal action on behalf of a police officer in Scotland. He was a worker in Fairfield's ship-yard and belonged to a social club there. As soon as he became a police officer, the committee barred him from the premises. After examining the rules of the club, they finally allowed him to continue as a member.' On the other hand, it is not unknown for a village to try to keep a particular local policeman. This sometimes worries senior officers, who wonder if this relationship is too close for the policeman to be able to enforce the law properly. The policeman's reply to that might well be: 'If the relationship is as it should be, the village exerts its own pressure, in support of you, so that, for the benefit of all, the law is not flouted. I am, after all, no more than a civilian in uniform.'

The more orthodox view is that, by keeping people at a distance, a policeman can enforce the law when he has to, without individual members of the public regarding this as a betrayal of a relationship. Some people try to get to know a policeman to make him more loyal to them than to his job. (A similar problem arises in a slightly different way in a policeman's relations with his informants.) It is a difficult balance to strike. The beat policeman has to be able to chat to people, so as to know what is going on. Because they know him as an individual, people in a village do not resent the fact that, living amongst them, he knows so much about them. They trust him. If the same amount of information were transferred into a computer's memory in some distant headquarters, they would feel it to be an infringement of their privacy.

(That the police are little different from any other group in their reactions is illustrated by protests at the Police Federation's annual conference in 1971 that files were being kept of personal details on individual policemen.)

Whereas the policeman in the country may find he has to put himself at a distance from the public, he is put at a distance in a big city by the anonymity of life there. There the public cannot so easily get to know a policeman on duty. The distance from the local populace makes the police seem more anonymous, with individual officers less responsive to public pressure, because this pressure is less continuous and more diffuse. In the city, moreover, because the officer knows fewer ordinary members of the public locally as individuals, it is less easy for him to take their personal foibles into account when opportunity arises to exercise his power of discretion. He is less able to be a respecter of persons. He has to judge more by appearances, and the results of this can sometimes be unfortunate, as we have seen.

An illustration of the way that police may hold stereotyped opinions about students was provided by Mr Roger Haworth, then president of the Students' Union at Aston

University, Birmingham. He told the Police Federation seminar in June, 1971: 'I walked into a police station the other day on business, and the officer behind the desk said, "So you're Haworth." Then a man walked in behind me who had short hair and a suit. The officer said, "Can I help you, sir?" ' For the young policeman, of course, there is a sharp contrast between his own, short-haired discipline, and what he may regard as the lax standards of his contemporaries who, although having more academic ability than he, and greater freedom of opportunity, seem to do more shouting about the lack of it.

There is also a much simpler and more obvious reason for a gap between the public and the police. The public know that the police are there to enforce the law and they are trained to be sceptical and suspicious. This brings out the guilt in people. One officer said: 'If I see somebody living it up suddenly, I can't help wondering where the money has come from.' One visitor to the Police College, Bramshill, had a similar experience. He saw a senior officer's eyes fall on a coat-hanger. The visitor had brought it with him, and it had the name of a firm on it. Anticipating the unspoken question, he explained what was true. The coat-hanger had been provided along with the suit.

The police, because they rely on the confidence of the public, are deeply sensitive about criticism, and sometimes this defensiveness makes them over-react to it. Perspective is gained by a look at their history. The public attitude includes a concern for liberty, which is deep-seated in Britain. Anything that has to regulate this liberty – whatever form that regulation takes – is bound to be questioned, and rightly so. This is part of the processes of a healthy democracy, which usually leads to fierce debate in Parliament about the introduction of laws which, of course, the police have afterwards to enforce.

Before the formation of the police, a Parliamentary Committee reported to the then Home Secretary, Sir Robert Peel:

'It is difficult to reconcile an effective system of police with that perfect freedom of action and exemption from interference which are the great privileges and blessings of society in this country, and your committee think that the forfeiture or curtailment of such advantages would be too great a sacrifice for improvements in police, or facilities in the detection of crime, however desirable in themselves, if abstractedly considered.'

Mr John Alderson, formerly Commandant of the Police College, Bramshill and now Chief Constable of Devon and Cornwall, comments: 'With Fouché (the notorious French police chief) as an example over the Channel, they saw the police as a greater evil than the flourishing of crime.'

The police came into being in 1829 after Peel made a political bargain with the City of London, in which City members of Parliament promised support for his establishment of the Metropolitan Force, provided they were able to have their own police in the City. Peel needed their support, as the idea had been killed once before. In Ireland he had established a preventive force on the lines of the gendarmerie in France. In Britain it was the citizen's job to keep the peace, rather than the government's. In 1833, four years after the establishment of the police, another Parliamentary Committee reported: 'It appears to your Committee that the Metropolitan Police has imposed no restraint upon public bodies or individuals which is not entirely consistent with the fullest practical exercise of every civil privilege, and with the most unrestrained intercourse of private society.'

The very words 'police constable' are an amalgam expressing the duality of the police role in enforcing the law and yet being no more than a representative in uniform of the public. This duality has put the police into a buffer position between state and public, maintaining contact with both sides. The word 'constable' is derived from the Latin *comes stabuli*, the Master of the Horse of the Eastern Emperors at Byzantium. John Deane Potter explains in *Scotland Yard*: 'From as early as 1252, one or more constables has been appointed for each parish in England. It was a position of honour, going to the men who today are local councillors, trade union officials, justices of the peace.' The word 'police', however, has associations more with the machinery of state. According to Brian Chapman in *Police State*, the Romans took over from the Greeks the term *politeia*, which became latinised as *politia*. It was a derivative from the Greek word *polis*, and the English words 'politics' and 'policy' come from this same root. The term *politeia* was a comprehensive one, touching on all matters affecting the survival and welfare of the inhabitants of the city. It comprised within itself the whole notion of 'the art of governing the city'.

The original nineteenth-century objection to the police – that they would spy on people and impair liberty – has echoes in various attitudes towards them today. In 1963 Holborn Borough Council turned down a recommendation of its highways committee that plain-clothes wardens should be employed to prevent meter-feeding, on the grounds that it would be 'distasteful'. There are similar objections to the use of hidden radar traps to catch speeding motorists, or of a helicopter for similar purposes. There are periodic fears expressed that television cameras installed, the police say, for traffic control in London, will be used to snoop on individuals. Sometimes the police are in a dilemma about the methods open to them in enforcing the law. A letter to *Autosport* once said: 'Sir, I would like to issue a warning to my fellow motorists who travel on the M.4. There is a certain Sunbeam Tiger that is being used for the ungentlemanly practice of catching 70 m.p.h. speed limit exceeders. It has absolutely no identification, so the Metropolitan Police must be having great fun. I wonder if Rootes (the manufacturers) approve of their vehicle being used in this way?' The police dilemma was solved by compromise. Although the car was anonymous, the burly crew were in uniform.

There is also a precedent for the mixed feelings, held by some, over the role of the police in connection with protest. It was the Gordon riots of 1780 in London which first made people seriously think about the need for a police force. Beginning as a protest against the repeal of anti-Catholic laws – at this stage it could have been nipped in the bud by a disciplined police force – the crowd was joined by a burning, murdering, looting mob. Troops called in to defend he city quelled the riot, but only after 200 people had been killed and 250 wounded by their shooting. Demands for a police force were countered by a fear that it would be merely a tool of the government.

This fear is something that the police have had to live down at times ever since, their task made the more difficult by the fact that they must remain silent on political matters, which makes them seem acquiescent to the needs of the establishment. Indeed, they were not allowed to vote in Parliamentary elections before 1887, or in local ones until 1893. Their disciplinary code prevents them from taking any active part in politics.

Certainly, they were regarded as a repressive arm of the government after 'Bloody Sunday', 13 November 1887. The London radicals were refused permission by the Commissioner of Police to use Trafalgar Square for a meeting, after previous incidents. They decided to go ahead, and such notables as William Morris and George Bernard Shaw took part. Shaw has described how, in the battle of the square, Robert Bontine Cunninghame Graham, a Scottish Socialist M.P., was personally and bodily assailed by the concerted military and constabulary forces .

Anne Fremantle, in *This Little Band of Prophets*, a book about the British Fabians, says: 'Graham and John Burns chained themselves to the railings of Morley's Hotel, and John Burns, waving the red flag, resisted the police and was battered. Baton charges were made by the police in Holborn and the Strand, and finally the foot and horse guards were called out and charged the crowd. Graham was hit over the head with a truncheon and bled profusely;

both he and Burns were arrested.' There were over 200 casualties, and two men later died of their injuries. Henry Salt, a prominent early Fabian and a master at Eton College, had his watch stolen, and later wrote sadly: 'I couldn't protest the conduct of the police in the square and invoke them against the pickpockets.' The dilemma created by the different roles of the police was never more succinctly expressed.

It is noticeable that often the stock of the police is at its lowest when protest is at its highest and the gap widest between sections of the public and the government. The events of Bloody Sunday were part of the developments that led eventually to the formation of the Labour Party, to close the gap between government and that section of the public which felt itself to be inadequately represented politically. The role of the police on these occasions is to subdue protest, so that it does not get out of hand. This makes sense only because, eventually, the British political system is flexible and sensitive enough to change, so that developing pressures can then be represented democratically. If this process were altered, by some hardening of the arteries of the British political system, the police would have an impossible task. This is why the keeping of public tranquillity is beyond their power alone. It depends upon the subtle interplay of politics. Recently, policemen have complained that they feel as if they are holding down the lid on a pressure cooker. The answer is for the government and Parliament to turn down the gas.

At the time of severe unemployment in the 1920s and 1930s the police were again cast into a buffer role. Again, through the subsequent application of modern economic theory and because of the political necessity of keeping down unemployment to an acceptable minimum, the pressures that the police had to control then have subsequently been reduced.

Ben Whitaker writes in his book *The Police*: 'Much of the resentment of the police in some districts (such as those parts of London and South Wales where they are still booed on the cinema screen) dates from the time of the hunger marches. It is diminishing (old songs like "We'll kill all the coppers who come down our way" have disappeared), but many mothers still teach their children to fear a policeman by using him as a threat for misbehaviour.'

Today, there are other people who talk rhetorically of 'killing a copper'. In the last three years, I have heard black men engaged in protest chant 'Kill the pigs'. One indeed told the Select Committee on Race Relations and Immigration: 'We must kill policemen.'

History is repeating itself, with black people cast in the role of the new working class. Again it appears that the police are in the middle as the gap between authority and people – in this case, young blacks – widens. Today it is the young black person who is most likely to be out of work when he leaves school, and in parts of the country young blacks have begun to get into trouble with the police.

Of course, this extreme reaction has to be seen in the context of more general attitudes of the public towards the police. A survey carried out for *The Times* by Opinion Research Centre and published on 30 April 1974 showed that only two of the leading British institutions enjoyed the unqualified confidence of most voters. The two were the police and the leaders of medicine.

Some of the latest systematic research into public attitudes was carried out in 1971 by Marketing Advisory Services as an aid to recruiting. Their report on the image of the police was made on behalf of the Home Office for the Central Office of Information. The findings, which are still unpublished, suggest that attitudes towards the police are more favourable than unfavourable. For instance, more people think that the police are respected than that they cause apprehension. The police provide an important service in protecting the citizen and helping him in times of trouble. But there is also some fear of the police and a feeling that they are down on young people and the unconventional. The most worrying feature was that this fear was displayed by about half of the general public sampled and up to two-thirds of younger age groups interviewed. It is also surprising that this fear was felt particularly among the educated young. The worst potential danger of these feelings and attitudes is that they could lead to the creation of a gap between the police and the public wide enough to undermine public co-operation, as people would be less eager to get in touch with the police.

Those who have studied the report argue, not entirely convincingly, that it is the multiplicity of laws that worries people, rather than the police who have to enforce them. But a feeling is apparent from the survey that the police do not much like people who wear way-out clothes and long hair. (In other words, the findings appear to tie up with the evidence of stereotyping we have discussed.)

There is an interesting echo in the report of the public attitudes of the last century before the formation of the police: that the fight against crime, although important, could take second place to other issues. The survey found that, although people regard the fight against crime as important, it comes second in their eyes to looking after the public and is a means to that wider end. Thus, when people think of the police, they have in mind mainly the uniformed man on the beat, rather than the detective.

According to the survey, the police feel that it is good that there is understanding of their difficulties and a willingness to put down criticism to the fact that they are undermanned and overworked. Some blame is attributed to the media for giving an unbalanced picture of the police.

While the survey examines part of the perspective of public opinion, another study by Mrs Monica Shaw and Mr W. Williamson, reported in *The Criminologist*, demonstrated that what the public expects of the police varies from area to area. People living in a predominantly middle-class area reacted favourably to the police on all counts. Such people are less likely to consider the police as vindictive or brutal than those living elsewhere, and are generally likely to be lenient with policemen breaking the rules.

As might be expected, people had different attitudes in a predominantly stable working-class community, and these attitudes were shared by people living in another working-class area which had a large turnover of residents. This latter district was populated by Indian and Pakistani immigrants and was, moreover, being rapidly developed under a slum clearance scheme. It bore all the marks of the run-down city environment in which many immigrant communities live. In both these areas, the survey found, people were more critical of the police and were more likely to report them if they broke the rules.

In a fourth area, mixed in class, with a lot of residential property and recently developed council estates, there was a mixed response, but clearly more criticism of the police than in the predominantly middle-class area.

Thus it seems that an area of the sort typically containing immigrants is likely to be most critical of the police. Further analysis shows that the lower down the social scale people are, the less likely they are to help the police and think them fair. Age has a lot to do with attitudes, regardless of area. The proportion in the 18–35 age group who respected the police was 61·7 per cent, compared with those in the 56-and-over age group, where the proportion was 92·9 per cent.

Furthermore, the authors say, it is clear that the type of contact between the police and the public differs according to the area and this difference contributes to variations in attitudes. In the predominantly middle-class area, which also accommodated a sizeable number of students, the proportion of people who reported having been stopped and questioned by the police was 9·1 per cent. In the mixed class residential and council-house area the figure was only 1·8 per cent. But in the stable working-class area the figure was 20·7 per cent; and in the shifting, run-down area being redeveloped and accommodating many immigrants, the proportion was 19·1 per cent. Other forms of contact, such as arrests and warnings, showed the same pattern.

Similarly, those who reported having been helped by the police were, in the middle-class area, 63·2 per cent; 56·6 per cent in the mixed-class area; 48 per cent in the stable working-class community; and 39·7 per cent in the run-down area with immigrants.

What these figures indicate, when considered in conjunction with a survey carried out for *The Times* by Marplan in 1970, is that the sort of person living in areas such as those in which immigrants have their homes is likely to have the most potentially abrasive contact with the police, particularly if the person living there is young.

The Marplan survey showed that two out of three young West Indians believed the police dealt with them unfairly. Expanding their reasons, 24 per cent said the police did not like coloured people, and 24 per cent said that the police beat up black people and handled them roughly. Another 14 per cent said that the police would pick them up for just walking or standing in a group. *Yet, surprisingly, 73 per cent of the West Indians interviewed by Marplan had never had any personal encounters with the police.* News of those who have spreads like wildfire through the community, and, for those black people who think badly of the police, such talk serves to substantiate their impression. The fact that they expect friction no doubt influences their own attitudes, and must in turn have an effect on police reactions, in a process of stereophonic amplification, in which, however, distortion obscures the still small voice of reason.

A major reason for the reputation of the police among sections of the black community rests on the common knowledge of a number of well-documented cases. Two of the best remembered involved diplomats. As the result of one of them, the Nigerian High Commission delivered what it called 'a strong protest note' to the Foreign Office. Police treatment of Mr Clement Gomwalk, First Secretary at the Commission, was 'unjustified and uncalled for', it said. Although Mr Gomwalk maintained that the Mercedes he had was his and offered to produce documentary evidence to that effect, he was not given a chance, the note added. 'Instead, he was grabbed and dragged out of his car into a waiting police-car. Once in the car he was hand-cuffed and beaten up while being taken to Brixton Police Station.' The note rejected 'the spirited defence of the brutal action by the British Home Secretary, Mr James Callaghan, as a negation of British justice by condemning Mr Gomwalk without hearing his side of the story.'

Mr Callaghan had told the House of Commons:

'Police inquiries took place on the morning of the 15th November about a car which was causing a serious obstruction in a "No Waiting" area in Brixton. The licence plate bore a different number from the road fund licence disc and there was a possibility that the vehicle might have been stolen. Mr Gomwalk, who was not known at this stage to be a diplomat, returned to the car, and refused to give any explanation of the ownership. During questioning by the police, a hostile crowd gathered, a struggle took place, and in order to prevent a breach of the peace, Mr Gomwalk was arrested and taken to Brixton Police Station. His identity and entitlement to diplomatic immunity were established while he was there and he was released. In the meantime, a disturbance developed as a result of which six other people were arrested, against whom proceedings are now pending. In the circumstances, it would not be proper for me to make any further comment.'

An inquiry conducted by a Metropolitan Police Chief Superintendent from another division 'disclosed a substantial conflict of evidence between Mr and Mrs Gomwalk and the police officers', said a Home Office statement. It had not been possible to resolve this discrepancy from the evidence of other witnesses. 'In the light of the investigating officer's report, the Commissioner of Police is unable to find that his officers acted otherwise than correctly and in accordance with their duty.'

In accordance with the Police Act 1964, the report on the investigation was referred to the Director of Public Prosecutions. He advised that the evidence did not warrant criminal proceedings against any of the officers about whom Mr Gomwalk had complained.

The Gomwalk case, which is among several described in detail by Derek Humphry in *Police Power and Black People*, raises a number of important issues. Firstly, from the police point of view, they are faced with an increasing number of stolen cars being imported to Britain from the Continent, and a Mercedes is obviously worth stealing and bringing in. Because of the lack of opportunity for black people to do well in British society, those who are able to afford to buy an expensive Mercedes are few and far between. Thus, suspicions were obviously aroused. But they arose because of the process of stereotyping. Secondly, black people are unlikely ever to be satisfied with the outcome of the inquiry, which was conducted by another Metropolitan Police Officer.

Many young black people believe that, if such trouble could happen to a diplomat like Mr Gomwalk – and this was not the only incident of its kind involving a black diplomat – it can happen to anybody. There were more misunderstandings after police one night stopped a private car in which Mr Reg Philips, then the Jamaican Deputy High Commissioner and a man of impeccable character who had done more than most for race relations in Britain, was a passenger. The result was that news of the incident reverberated angrily in the West Indian community and there was further criticism of the police who would, no doubt, say that they were acting from the best of motives. Distrust of the police is widespread among young black people.

Yet is it not enough merely to record this fact, and accept it or reject it. The reasons are worth exploring in greater depth, as will be done in Section II.

3 Traffic and the Environment

The police carry the can for the government –
good police-work conceals the true causes of trouble –
the crucial difference between 'law' and 'order' –
motoring anarchy – traffic control on a knife-edge –
bad buildings cause crime

In many ways the problems faced by the police, and their reaction to them, are epitomised by traffic and its control. But as with crime and public turbulence, the police can seek to deal only with the effects. The causes are usually beyond their control.

Traffic has to be seen as part of a much wider canvas. Its growth, and the complexity of the problems it poses, are symptoms of the increasing pace, not only of life, but also of change. To make way for the motor-car, and the motorways it demands, landscapes have been bulldozed and the environment – which is widely recognised as part of the cause of crime – changed. Whatever the government – local or national – decrees in the way of regulations, new roads, pedestrian precincts and bus lanes, it is the police who have to deal with the results and make the system work.

The problem is already sizeable. Because the subject is not very glamorous and makes little news, it comes as a surprise that between 10 and 12 per cent of total police effort is now spent in dealing with traffic, although, in the course of that activity, officers will also deal with other police tasks. In Britain during 1970 there was a road death every seventy minutes and a non-fatal casualty every eighty-nine seconds. Each case makes inroads into police time.

The total number of road accidents for the year was more than 267,000; 7,500 people died and 93,500 were injured seriously. Nearly one in four casualties is a pedestrian and 95 per cent of all pedestrian casualties occur in built-up areas. The figures can be given some sort of perspective if one were to substitute the words 'death by violence' for death by road accident. If someone were said to have died every seventy minutes through violent injury, the impact on the public mind might be greater. Indeed, Sir Robert Mark said on 20 February 1973 that Londoners were in greater peril from traffic than from crime.

Research done by Birmingham University suggests that the extent to which the individual is responsible for violent death on the roads is great. Of course, it is seldom that an accident has a single cause. It is more usually the result of the combined effects of deficiencies in the vehicle-user, the vehicle itself, the road lay-out, or road surface. These deficiencies may be accentuated by the time of the day and the weather.

The University's study suggests that causes can be split up as follows:

Factors involved	*per cent*
Environment	4·3
Vehicle	4·3
Road-user	44·7
Environment/vehicle	1·0
Vehicle/road-user	7·1
Environment/road-user	31·0
Environment/vehicle/road-user	7·6
	100·0

In other words, road-users contribute in some way, at least in part, to over 90 per cent of the accidents. The individual's role is important. He is subjected to great pressure. On average he has to cope with ten or more highway and traffic events every second; two or more driver observations a second; one to three driver decisions every second; 30-120 driver actions per minute; at least one driver error every two minutes; a hazardous situation every hour or two; a near collision twice a month.

In the last twenty years road traffic has trebled, whereas road casualties have doubled. But road deaths have increased by 57 per cent over a period when population has increased by about 10 per cent and the odds against losing one's life on the roads have shortened from 150:1 to 100:1. Britain is fortunate insofar as it had 14 deaths per 100,000 population in 1969, compared with 27 in the U.S.A., 32 in France and 27 in Germany.

The point this demonstrates is that, whatever the police do, the maintenance of public tranquillity on the roads and the prevention of offences is clearly a task beyond them alone, as with other areas of police work. The creation of better road systems on the outskirts of London, for example, to draw traffic on to circular routes, instead of routing it through the centre, would reduce traffic jams and reduce some of the frustration that can lead to accidents and bad driving. All the police can do is, by the enforcement of regulation and re-routing, to reduce the possibility of hold-ups and accidents. As with the maintenance of public tranquillity in the political field, all the police can hope to do is hold down the lid on the pressure cooker. It is for Parliament and government, local as well as national, to turn down the gas. A lot also depends upon the individual driver and pedestrian.

Indeed, there is a case for saying that the better the police do their job, the less the true causes of trouble, real or potential, become apparent. The better that they control political demonstrations, for example, the less dramatic these are; and the less publicity they receive, the less will attention be focused on the true causes of discontent, when the purpose of the demonstration is to draw attention to them. Similarly with traffic: the better the police keep it moving within an existing system, the less the faults of that system become apparent. In general, government departments are not very forward-looking. They depend much upon the in-tray principle. Unless problems come into the in-tray they tend not to be given much priority. Another way of expressing this is to say that 'the political will is not there'. The underlying political principle is – to put it cynically – that the government will not take action unless failure to do so causes a bigger row than if they had taken action. It is a great reason for doing nothing. The policeman standing on the corner directing traffic away from its shortest, most favoured route because of some hold-up caused by the inadequate road system is not a very popular figure. Rather as, for example, the policeman in Notting Hill is made by black people the scape-goat of authority that has failed to act over atrocious social conditions, so are the traffic police the nearest target for discontent.

One of the main principles behind traffic policing – the same principle underlying much else of police work in Britain – is of such importance that without it law and order would collapse: the principle of self-control.

Self-control is never far away from traditional law enforcement in this country. It is epitomised by the queue. There is, of course, no law covering queues in general, but observers looking at the British might conclude that there could be. The principle behind it is, put at its simplest, first come, first served. So strong is public belief in this principle that the Conservative Government in the early 1970s was able to use it to political effect. Asians with U.K. passports and deprived of their livelihood in Tanzania – indeed, sometimes of their right to be there – set off for Britain without proper entry papers, only to be sent back again on arrival or thrown into gaol until their cases had been examined. The government's reason, calculated to win public support, was that they were 'queue-jumpers'.

In some provincial cities motorists respect the idea of a queue so much that, even where there is room for two lines of vehicles waiting at traffic lights, vehicles, instead, form one queue. The motorist who tries to sneak up the side of a single line of traffic is regarded as breaking the informal rules, and is liable to be hooted at or to find a vehicle asserting its right over him by trying to prevent him from overtaking. In London, where the principle of give and take is more flexibly practised, people become indignant less easily. Although such informal enforcement of the law can in certain circumstances be dangerous – for instance, if a line of traffic closes up and the overtaking motorist finds himself marooned in the face of oncoming traffic – police do rely upon it.

That is why small traffic islands have in some places replaced traffic lights at junctions, so that they are 'self-policing'. In other words, motorists arriving at a junction decide for themselves when it is safe to emerge into the circling traffic stream. People finding themselves involved in minor collisions on roads may discover that the police are not very interested unless some offence has been committed, or injury has occurred, or traffic is held up; it remains the responsibility of the people involved to exchange names and addresses for insurance purposes. An accident in Britain is greeted with a calm that seems almost deliberate in contrast with the arm-waving and general vehemence in, say, Italy.

Whenever streets are closed as pedestrian precincts or bus lanes are created, the police hope that the effects will be self-policing, although the responsibility for making them work is theirs. In London computer systems linked to traffic lights are concerned with the flow and density of traffic so that vehicles do not get snarled up. Frustration can be dangerous.

The British, however, have never been so orderly when a diminution of their personal freedom has been involved. The weakness of demands for 'law-and-order' is that its advocates lump together two concepts that are not exactly similar. Only the lawless would object to the general principle of the rule of law, provided that it is applied fairly ('a fair cop' is an old cliché). But the rule of order would get a very different response.

The pedestrian in this country, even more than the motorist, believes in freedom of movement, and does not like it if demands for apparently unnecessary order restrict it. The point at which law hardens into order can be a sore one. Traces of a thin red line can still be seen beside the pavement in Fleet Street as evidence of a futile attempt to control pedestrians. These were part of an experiment in which pedestrians were to be allowed to cross the street only at the points which authority indicated. The public was treated to the spectacle of elderly businessmen waiting until a policeman's back was turned and then, risking life and reputation, delightedly hopping over the line and back again in a vigorous response to a challenge. But in Sweden, on the day that traffic switched from left-hand to right-hand drive, the populace allowed itself to be very strictly controlled, crossing streets when they were told and only at selected points. In Denmark, too, pedestrians wait for traffic lights to tell them when to cross roads, even when there is no traffic about.

Another general principle of policing which we have considered and which applies to traffic is that the less action that is taken by the government to alleviate causes of potential trouble, the more difficult becomes the police task in controlling that trouble. Anarchy could then result. Traffic in London provides a disturbing example. The police and traffic wardens simply have not the resources to enforce the law against the numbers of people who break it. The freedom demanded by some motorists to park where they wish, despite the presence of restrictions, has become anarchic, and the right of other individuals in the community at large to free movement is impaired as a result.

London's traffic has been on a knife-edge. Research and experience have shown that, if any of the major intersections on the inner ring road are blocked, it is only a matter of minutes before the next important junction is overrun. The shortest breathing space at the Angel junction is ninety seconds. There is three minutes' grace at Marble Arch. Congestion, thereafter, becomes cumulative and in general it takes much longer to disperse a queue than it takes one to form. Some examples of traffic congestion are as follows:

20 April 1972 – a serious fire in Blackwall Tunnel, London, resulted in a closure of the northbound tunnel for a day. Widespread congestion in the south-east and eastern areas persisted until beyond the afternoon peak.

27 September 1972 – the northbound Blackwall tunnel was closed for six hours when a barge sank on top of the underwater structure.

September 1972 – traffic came to a standstill for more than six hours throughout the central area of London in one of the worst examples of traffic congestion there ever. The cause was a combination of very heavy afternoon peak traffic, heavy rain, several accidents and a broken down bus.

In such circumstances, where a single vehicle in the wrong place can help to produce chaos, the price that society pays for the freedom of the individual driver to park where he likes is very high. Unfortunately, the enforcement system is so overloaded that many of the £2 fixed penalties for parking offences are evaded. Over a million are issued each year in London alone.

A breakdown of fixed penalty notices issued in April 1972, is as follows:

Issued	96,721
Paid	
– within 21 days	20,504
– late	35,709

Written off
  – voluntarily

Diplomatic privilege	2,892
Visitors	7,430
Warden resigned	50
Mitigating circumstances	2,773
Traffic Warden error	2,373

  – involuntarily

Unable to trace driver	854
Statutory time	23,364

Summonses 772

Those whom the police term 'high repeat evaders' are extremely difficult to trace and identify by door-to-door inquiries. Nearly half of the fixed penalty notices issued in the month examined had to be written off for one reason or another. The biggest proportion (23,364, a huge number) were because the statutory time had elapsed.

Some high repeat evaders do pay the fixed penalties, and often ask that they should not be troubled with postal and personal visits about them. One business executive will sometimes telephone the local traffic wardens' centre to say that he is going abroad shortly and to ask the amount outstanding. He pays about £50 a month. Another, when faced with single inquiries, is usually very indignant, considers his time wasted and asks for fortnightly visits. He never checks the list of notices presented to him, and in 1972 paid well over £300. One agency has, over the past four years, paid an average of £70 monthly, and also for twenty removal charges. Some companies pay for their employees' penalties.

Clearly the police have an impossible task when people do not respect the law and exercise self-control – the only way in which the law can work in a society where it is not repressive. The police can be effective only if there is a consensus at work within the community, and in traffic there clearly is not.

While the growth of traffic, without adequate planning to cope with it, is inducing a form of anarchy, the problem has to be seen in a broader context. The traffic crisis is part of a more general malaise, caused by the pace of environmental change, that has been disorientating people and uprooting communities.

The pace of change is increasing. Alvin Toffler in *Future Shock* says:

'In 1850, only four cities on the face of the earth had a population of one million or more. By 1900, the number had increased to 19. But by 1960, there were 141, and today urban population is rocketing upwards at a rate of 6.5 per cent per year, according to Edgar de Vries and J. P. Thysse of the Institute of Social Science in the Hague. This single, stark statistic means a doubling of the earth's urban population within 11 years.

'One way to grasp the meaning of change on so phenomenal a scale is to imagine what would happen if all existing cities, instead of expanding, retained their present size. If this were so, in order to accommodate the new urban millions we would have to build a duplicate city for each of the hundreds that already dot the globe. A new Tokyo, a new Hamburg, a new Rome and Rangoon – and all within 11 years.'

This of course changes the nature of the society that the police have to deal with. Rural areas, which change slowly, are comparatively easy to police, in terms of enforcing the law when it is broken, largely because communities regulate themselves – they 'self-police' by exerting pressures on people to conform – and people and their characteristics are known, and they can be more easily traced. Cities are places where people can remain anonymous and hide. Pressures upon people to conform are less, and are further reduced by the redevelopment of old 'village-type' communities and the scattering of people into tall blocks.

In Britain people have also dispersed from inner cities to new towns. New town 'blues', as they have been called, symptomised by vandalism and other troubles, indicate the teething troubles met in creating new communities. Psychiatrists are well aware of the effect of moving people from old familiar surroundings and friends, of their losing the support of their old community in times of stress, and also of missing the need to conform to an accepted pattern of behaviour within the new community. The sense of isolation can be increased if a family, particularly with young children, is moved into a block of high-rise flats. Research and interviews carried out with people living in such flats have shown the pressures upon them to be high, particularly upon mothers and young children. Mothers are afraid to allow their children to play at ground level, out of sight and without supervision, and there may not always be facilities anyway. In high-rise flats neighbours tend to complain if children are noisy. Some mothers notice how children run wild when occasionally taken to a nearby park. Some experts have blamed violent behaviour by youngsters on the inadequacy of recreational facilities: they have nowhere to let off steam.

It is easy to see how, in such circumstances, criminal tendencies are formed. In the London Borough of Brent on 29 March 1973 the Select Committee of Race Relations and Immigration was told that children in tall blocks of flats found themselves at a disadvantage on going to school. Because of their isolation the children had not learnt to speak properly or how to play. In the freer atmosphere of school they were at a loss and under stress. School teachers had to teach them simple words to speak before they could begin to read.

The environment in which these children are being brought up is of the type likely to cause them to turn to crime against the community, because they failed, in their formative years, to learn proper, sustained relationships with other people. Community is not respected, because it means nothing.

Their lack of opportunity for playing together makes it difficult not only for them to socialise, but also to verbalise. Verbalisation of aggression is a way of expressing it and getting it out of the system. Those who cannot verbalise it may express aggression in other ways, perhaps physically. Treatment in Grendon Underwood psychiatric prison concentrates on teaching men, some of them potentially violent, how to relate to each other in what is called the therapeutic community. One of the symptoms of psychopathy is that the aggressor is not concerned about the effects of his actions upon others. In a therapeutic community, where there are meetings in which individuals' actions are discussed and their places in that community depend upon this, they begin to temper their actions to the community's good.

Dr Mary Ellis, senior medical officer at Feltham Borstal, told a conference of the National Association for the Care and Resettlement of Offenders in Bristol on 14 June 1972 that part of the reason for violence was often that delinquent young people were unable to put their frustration into words. Instead, they acted it out. Today, in the modern, urban, concrete setting, where actions are carefully regulated, there is not much opportunity for children to 'act out' without getting into trouble. Henry Fielding's Tom Jones, the subject of a novel of that name, was a boisterous, harum-scarum lad, always in trouble, but at least he had the chance to let off steam in the countryside on horse-back. Today's equivalent in the urban setting might conceivably be the ton-up kids, their motor-cycles roaring to impress their girlfriends as a kind of mating call in the concrete jungle.

The link between crime and vandalism on the one hand and high-rise architecture on the other has been most closely studied in New York. Commander Peter Marshall, when head of Scotland Yard's crime prevention department, studied a scheme there to overcome the worst effects of some types of housing design. The scheme was based on a preliminary report to the New York Housing Authority of an analysis of 100 of the Authority's housing projects. This showed that larger projects experienced more crime than smaller ones. A group of large projects, with 1,000 dwelling units or more, selected at random, had a higher mean crime rate than a group of small projects in 99 out of 100 samples.

In one scheme tenants were to be provided with closed-circuit television sets to get a view of lobbies, entrances and lifts, when they expected visitors or children. The hope was that this would work like a series of windows, helping residents to keep a watch over their 'territory'. Other changes included the dividing up of the barren wastes between tall blocks into small areas so that neighbours could converse and get to know each other.

If some of the new housing estates lack community spirit, older housing, too, when decayed and neglected by the authorities, causes trouble that the police have to sort out. In Notting Hill on 10 February 1972 the Select Committee on Race Relations and Immigration was told by Commander G. E. H. Maggs: 'If all these people could be lifted out of this environment and put in a more desirable neighbourhood, many of the problems would disappear.' Social conditions in some parts were very bad, he said, and the police service was the only visible and tangible form of authority.

The effect of the environment in this respect is well summed up by Mr Hugh Klare, former secretary of the Howard League and of the Division of Crime Problems in the Council of Europe. He has contrasted anonymous cities with tribal life, in which rituals abound and in which there is a safe and physical outlet, even when behaviour is charged with strong and sometimes violent emotions. He writes in the book *Europe Tomorrow* that, in comparison, life in industrial cities in Europe is emotionally arid and without sufficient outlets. Many social institutions in large, complex, industrial societies do not reflect people's real needs and aspirations, he says. In such a competitive society, the least adequate cannot succeed at all and often turn to crime.

Thus there is a consistent thread running through the problems of the police and the attitude of the public towards them. The police cannot fulfil their original objectives as well as many of them would wish, because of circumstances beyond their control. As experience in rural situations shows, the police sometimes put themselves at a distance from the public, quite deliberately, to make their job easier. But the pace and nature of modern social change not only causes some of the crime or contributes towards it, but may put police at such a distance from the public that their role becomes difficult. Within the creaking structure of the city, originally designed to cope with a more leisurely, horse-drawn era, traffic offences are an example of the way in which anarchy can result when the consensus that contributes to law and order is lost. The self-control of the public, and steady, reassuring contact with the police is essential to their effectiveness and understanding all round.

Without knowledge of individuals, the police and sections of the public tend to become stereotyped in each others' eyes. Obviously, there is no single view of the police. Opinion tends to depend upon the contact that an individual has with the police, the area in which he or she lives, and the social class to which he or she belongs. Coloured people, especially the young, live in the sort of areas and are in the age group in which contact is likely to be most abrasive. The biggest potential area of friction is with black youngsters. Social background contributes towards this friction, as it does to the other incidents which demand police attention.

The public and Parliament (which makes the laws) and the courts which administer them, help to define what role the police have. The police, by use of their powers of discretion in enforcing the law, try to strike a balance between the various conflicting pressures. Their reputation seems to be at its lowest when the gap between government and people is greatest, and when social pressures which cause people to protest have yet to find a political solution. How the police react to these pressures, and how they use their powers of discretion, depends also upon their own view of their role, and the development of new resources which enables them to carry it out. Much depends upon the nature of the police themselves, both as individuals and as a group. We shall examine this in the next chapter.

II
THE NATURE
OF THE POLICE

4 The Police Community

The shortage of black policemen – rejecting the
too-authoritarian recruit – conformist policemen –
the difficulties of leadership – the police as a minority –
their 'tribal' dialect and Victorian traditions –
attitudes towards outsiders.

There is a sign up in a West London hostel for homeless black youngsters anxious to find their role in society. The notice says: 'Who am I? What am I? Where am I going?' The same questions could well be asked of the police.

To judge from the number of times that subjects such as 'The role of the police in a changing society' figure at conferences, seminars and courses, it would appear that the police are themselves anxious to discover the answers. They invite along some of their most outspoken critics, provided that they are not so politically intransigent that a sterile confrontation results. The Police Federation has been constructive in its efforts to bridge the different points of view by providing opportunity for them to be expressed and debated with a police audience. The most far-sighted policemen and those with the most open minds benefit most.

Such attempts at understanding may meet with as much opposition among sections of the police as among, say, the more militant black power circles. Many policemen do not see why they should offer the olive branch of understanding to groups that attack them. Similarly, among the more militant of critics, whether black or white, there is a reluctance to be seen as a friend of the police.

This is why police efforts to recruit coloured people into the force have been frustrated. There are only 24 in the Metropolitan Force and 76 in Britain as a whole. Ask black youngsters why there are not more, and the answer is likely to be that joining the police would be going over to the enemy. In fact there are, as we shall see, more similarities between the police and some of the immigrant communities than either might care to admit. But to get to the heart of police attitudes about community relations, crime, and the police role, it is necessary first to ask: 'Who and what are the police?'

The simple answer is that there are no more than 100,000 policemen in England and Wales, backed up by 6,500 traffic wardens and 29,500 civilians. Included in the total are 20,000 Metropolitan policemen, 1,870 traffic wardens and 11,500 civilians. The fact that there is not a need for many more policemen is because the police have the support of the public, although this support tends to lessen among sections of the public when the gap between them and the government is widest.

Policemen come from a variety of backgrounds. There is at least one member of the nobility serving as a policeman, but by and large they are lower middle class or respectable working class, not usually educationally brilliant, though possessing, many of them, unusual astuteness. Of the 108 graduates in the Metropolitan Police in mid-1973 (99 men and 9 women), only 14 men and 1 woman had joined the Force under the graduate entry scheme.

The Metropolitan Force has introduced a set of new tests for would-be entrants known, rather formidably, as 'the police initial recruitment test battery' – a term reflecting the employment of psychologists in drawing it up. The tests have been devised by the Civil Service Department research division and the Force's principal psychologist. If the recruit has two GCE 'A' level passes or four 'O' level passes, which must include English language and mathematics, he is exempt from part of the tests. All have to do a social attitude test. Part of the reason for this, as given by senior officers, is to weed out the too authoritarian personality. The police seem to be looking for the man in the middle who is neither too authoritarian nor too permissive. Though the recruit is often pretty average in education and outlook, he has to be above average physically. Generally the minimum height for a policeman is 5 ft 8 ins. In one Welsh-speaking area of Wales, the then Chief Constable told me he was in a dilemma, caused by a shortage of suitable Welsh-speaking recruits. He could get enough tall English speakers, but, if he wanted more Welsh speakers, he had to lower the regulation height.

A Home Office Working Group was appointed to consider and recommend a standard entrance examination intended for adoption by police forces. Each chief officer has set, subject to the regulations, his own test. One chief officer, who had a highly systematic selection procedure, nevertheless once said: 'I would always reject a man with dirty, untrimmed finger-nails.' Cleanliness, obedience and punctuality is built into the police disciplinary code. Guests at police training establishments are likely to find boot polish and brushes ready for them in a drawer.

If accepted, the recruit does an initial training course which teaches him the essentials of law, court procedure and police practice, though the curriculum has been criticised for concentration on this form of encyclopaedic knowledge at the expense of a more general understanding of what makes society and people tick. Nevertheless, there are lectures which seek to broaden this understanding, and training increasingly has this in mind. Faced with a technical difficulty these days, the young policeman can quickly get advice over the personal radio. So encyclopaedic knowledge is not now quite so necessary. The recruit who survives the initial training course is then on probation for two years, during which his knowledge is being topped up by lectures. After those two years, the policeman is confirmed in his appointment.

Thus the average policeman is not likely to be known for his way-out views. Whatever his political opinions may be, the selection procedures ensure that the police force retains its conservative (with a small 'c') reputation. This is hardened by the strong traditions of the police and the natural scepticism of the policeman, which is used to cut down to size colleagues who do not conform. As is obvious from their reactions to each other and to outsiders, the average policeman distrusts theories, which are inclined to be regarded as 'woolly', and places great store, instead, on being 'practical'. The highest tribute that can be paid to a superior is that he is 'a good practical copper'.

One senior officer with this reputation used it as a sort of currency with which to lead his men. He commanded men in an area well known for its sensitive race relations. He knew that the more highly his men regarded him as 'one of us – a good practical copper', the more power of command he had in 'the bank', as he put it. He fostered it by appealing to qualities his men respected, among them an innate conservatism, by referring to finger-prints as 'that new-fangled device'. His riding boots he referred to jocularly as 'jack-boots'. He was looked upon with some affection as 'a character'. The more of this reputation as a practical copper he had 'in the bank' with his men, the further he could go in a progressive liberal direction. He arranged the posting out of the area of some men, not because he felt that they were bad policemen, but that race relations required an aptitude – just as did CID work or driving a patrol car – that they did not possess sufficiently. He said that his 'bank balance' of reputation dwindled and he was living on overdraft after one of his policemen was seriously injured in an incident involving a West Indian. He had what he termed 'an eye-ball to eye-ball confrontation' with some of his men, allowing them to speak their minds. They told him that soft policies were to blame for their colleague being injured.

Though he argued his point of view and was still able to exert a strong influence over his men, morale suffered. Policemen tend to regard an attack on one as an attack on all, and firmly close ranks when it happens. The dangers of a situation in which both the police and black people have closed ranks are obvious. In this instance, by a combination of straight talking and good leadership, a crisis was averted. He restored his 'bank balance' of good reputation with his men as 'a practical copper', and was then able to introduce some more liberal measures. The event which once more endeared him to his men was the way in which he immediately stood by an officer whose actions during an incident in which he was wounded by criminals were the subject of public controversy. The senior officer's reactions to the incident were instinctive and not calculated simply to win approval.

The example illustrates that a senior officer with a command in the police force is in a position rather similar to that of, say, a top trade unionist or even a black leader. They must not go so far ahead of the opinion of the men they represent that they lose contact with grass-roots and, with it, trust and support. In the case of the police, the sense of rank and file unity is increased by attacks from outside, whether physical or verbal. The police look after their own. They expect their leadership generally to stand by them, as a group. and these loyalties sometimes make it difficult for the police to accept self-criticism, except on their own terms. One senior officer on a course at Bramshill told me: 'Don't forget we're a tribe; we're a minority.' Other senior officers to whom the point has been put have not disagreed with it.

This comment opens a new vista of understanding of the police and in particular their attitude towards relationships with other groups in society and to the changes they are facing. Can it be supported by the facts? If the police can be regarded as a sub-group within society with its own culture, clearly this is more closely knit by kinship groups within it. These are remarkable. An astonishing number of officers come from families in which fathers, grandfathers, uncles, brothers and even sisters have been in the police. Mr Colin Woods, head of the CID at Scotland Yard, is the son of a policeman and his brothers also joined the police. In response to a paragraph in *Police Review*, Mr Frederick Bentley wrote how his great-great-grandfather, Joshua William Fitch Bentley, retired from Hull City Police in 1846. Mr Bentley's great-great-grandfather on his mother's side was a sergeant in the old Buckinghamshire Constabulary, and is believed to have been the first detective sergeant there. Mr Bentley continues: 'My father served in the old Reading Borough Police Force as a constable with the late Mr Carter, former Chief Constable of the old Windsor Borough Police Force, and this can be confirmed by his son, Mr Cyril Carter, until his retirement a few years ago Chief Constable of York.' Mr Bentley says that he himself joined the Essex Constabulary in April 1935, and resigned in 1946. His only son, Keith Bentley, is a serving officer in the Thames Valley Police Force. Although the Bentley family service with the police is exceptional, police officers say that other long records of family connections with the service abound.

Not only do the police have strong kinship ties, but they also have their own dialect. Some of the terms, like 'villain' and 'manor', used in the Metropolitan Police, seem to echo a feudal origin. Others, such as 'snow-drop', have contemporary meaning. It is used in Scotland and some other places to describe the kinky theft of women's underwear from a clothes line. 'Feeling collars' is what 'practical coppers' are expected to be able to do if arrest is resisted, and offenders have to be restrained forcibly.

The use of such terms, when applied to police work, reveals something of the police attitude towards it and other officers. 'A uniform carrier' is simply a policeman who does little except what he is told, and does not put himself out. While social reformers are understanding of the right of hippies and tramps to drop out of society, the police term for them is 'slag'. A CID officer who cuts corners through regulations is known as 'swift'. 'Putting oneself about', on the other hand, is to try and show off a bit, something which police do not like very much in their colleagues. This is demonstrated when long-serving Inspectors on courses try to cut down to size any member out to impress by flashing his knowledge at his colleagues' expense.

Graduates working with 'practical coppers' do not always find the going easy, as they do not easily fit in with the sceptical average bobby. Graduates of the special course at the Police College, Bramshill, are sometimes called 'five-day wonders'.

Some of the terms quoted here have been coined to describe behaviour which is regarded as not quite in tune with the *mores* of the police community. It is illuminating to consider meanings opposite to those of the terms cited, for they should very much reflect what policemen admire in themselves and other people have come to expect. The opposite of a 'uniform carrier' is someone who is willing to think for himself a bit and put himself out. If slag is vitreous smelting refuse, the opposite is purer raw material for something of use to society. The opposite of 'swift' is going more slowly and methodically which, while it may not bring about spectacular success, is an honest way of getting a job done well within the regulations; it is no coincidence that the police term for the much under-rated policeman on the beat doing his duties conscientiously is 'P.C. Plod'.

So the picture begins to emerge of a group of men suspicious of the untoward (as, indeed, their job demands), with their own limits of permissible behaviour, and rather traditionalist in outlook. In fact, the character of the police is well summed up by the titles of Samuel Smiles's books – *Self-help, Character, Thrift* and *Duty*. Self-help – the opposite to 'carrying a uniform' – is what every policeman is supposed to be able to practise. Apart from any other reason, the education system has disgorged him when he may not be particularly well-qualified and, within the Force, he has the opportunity to better himself, if he wishes to gain promotion. The fact that the police make so much more of the abilities of their men than the educational system is able to is more an indictment of the educational system than of the misleadingly low paper qualifications that some recruits have. Self-reliance, as well as the ability to work in a team, is also essential. 'Character' is something looked for in every recruit and candidate for promotion, while a strong sense of duty – to the Force and to society – is what distinguishes the police service as a whole. If police see one of their number becoming a big spender, they wonder where the money is coming from. With police pay as it is, thrift is essential.

It is significant that the virtues that Samuel Smiles was extolling were Victorian. They linger on in the police service. One senior police officer told me: 'Our Victorianism is a fortress we retreat into in times of trouble.' He described the original aims and objects of the police as being 'the old Testament'. The Force regulations are known as 'the Bible'. Forces contain certain fundamentalist and rather old-fashioned senior officers who swear by it. Other policemen sometimes hark back to Victorian codes of behaviour. Mr Frederick Drayton Porter, Chief Constable of Mid-Anglia, called for a return to Victorian courting manners by undergraduates at Cambridge. He said that, if they escorted their girl friends safely back to their colleges, it would help to obviate the risk of the girls being attacked.

This sense of tradition often comes out in police attitudes. For instance, the blue lamp which used to shine from the old police station at Paddington has been installed at the new one in Edgware Road. Eighty-one of the 195 Metropolitan police stations in use when this book was prepared were built before 1910. Though policemen like to be thought modern in outlook, they do not object as much as they might to working in cramped, out-of-date conditions. 'We rather like our old nicks,' said one policeman when I put it to him that, really, those old places, with their inadequate facilities and, in some cases, lack of proper security, were a hindrance rather than a help. Sometimes, it is astonishing how little, fundamentally, has changed.

The point is amply demonstrated by a visit to Thames Division at Wapping, to retrace the steps of the journalist who had written an article about policing the River

Thames in the first edition of *Strand Magazine* in 1891 and to see what similarities still remain. He wrote: 'The traditional blue lamp projects over a somewhat gloomy passage leading down to the river-side landing stage.' It has not changed much. The police station is set amongst the tall, gaunt warehouses of the docks. The lamp is outside, exactly as it was described in the first edition of the *Strand Magazine*. There has since been an extension to one side of the main room of the police station. Upstairs, off-duty officers still play billiards in a billiards room: one was mentioned by the reporter in 1891.

The boats were then rowed by 'three sturdy fellows under the charge of an Inspector'. In the powerful patrol boat on a comparable visit in 1972 were two sturdy fellows under an Inspector. As the engine roared and we slid away from the landing stage, the radio cackled out a police message about a disturbance in a public house south of the river. The *Strand* had said about the police station:

'Just in a crevice by the window are the telegraph instruments. A clicking noise is heard, and the Inspector hurriedly takes down on a slate a strange but suggestive message: "Information received of a prize fight for £2 a side, supposed to take place between Highgate and Hampstead." What has Highgate or Hampstead to do with the neighbourhood of Wapping, or how does a prize fight affect the members of the Thames police, who are anything but pugilistically inclined? In our innocence we learnt that it is customary to telegraph such information to all the principal stations throughout London. The steady routine of the Force is to be admired.'

The steady routine continues, though obviously developed with the use of modern equipment, and modern methods. The *Strand* reporter wrote: 'Still, the river policeman's eye and the light of his lantern are always searching for suspicious characters and guilty looking craft.'

On the night of the visit in 1972, the beam of a powerful search-light probed the nooks and crannies of the Thames. As the launch glided down stream to Greenwich, the pencil of light sought out barges. The name on each was read out and ticked off a list. The patrol took a good look at a sleek yacht with its masts down and concluded that it was being shipped out legitimately. The patrol noted a catamaran moored near one of the huge warehouses that had been turned into flats.

Strand Magazine described how Waterloo Bridge had become known as 'The Bridge of Sighs'. The article added: 'The dark water looks inviting to those burdened with toil and trouble, a place to receive those longing for rest and yearning for one word of sympathy.' Waterloo and Westminster Bridges remain favourites for people wishing to commit suicide by jumping into the river.

Minor changes apart, the job remains the same. Generally in the police service, the Victorian background and its continuing influence provide a store of experience to be handed on to the young policeman. There are also dangers, in that the police may become so set in their ways that even beneficial change may be resisted. 'Whoever heard of a computer feeling collars?' one policeman commented when talking about the latest impact of science on police work. A technologist who had had some contact with the police and their attitude towards the cost of computers said rather cruelly: 'The trouble is, they are so set in their ways that when they are talking of the cost of a computer they think in terms of boot equivalents.' This is no doubt unfair to a lot of policemen eager for change, but it may be no coincidence that courses intended as 'mind-broadening' are very much in vogue.

This sense of togetherness – of community spirit – is of value in providing a sense of comradeship and support for the policeman doing a difficult job. But Maureen Cain has pointed out in *Society and the Policeman's Role* that 'city policemen tend to divide society into the police and the rest, the public. And the public, too, was broadly subdivided into the "rough" and the "respectable" and within these categories by race and sex.' She comments: 'The division of the public into these categories enhances the *possibility* of police violence. Identification and therefore empathy is with certain categories only; the corresponding distancing of the other categories could enhance their vulnerability to rough treatment.'

She quotes an example in which over an hour was spent by police trying to find the address of a party an American air force officer wanted to go to, but a homeless coloured man was turned away from the station three times in one night without any advice as to where he could find accommodation.

Some thinking police officers recognise the dangers. One of the too few graduates in the police, Chief Inspector Jennifer Hilton, of the Metropolitan Police, who studied psychology, writes in *The Police We Deserve*, a collection of essays: 'A police officer may feel less constrained by normal patterns of behaviour if the people he is dealing with are vagrants or some other outcast group such as hippies or drug addicts that society (as he knows it), treats with little respect.' She also provides what is probably the key to a good deal of police behaviour. 'Few people are willing in a closed community, such as the police service, to express opinions or beliefs that are at variance with those of their colleagues. Not only group norms of behaviour are established but also stereotyped opinions about class and race.'

Chief Inspector Hilton's reading of the police attitudes is different from that which the police usually portray as their outlook. She says the police behavioural norms that are generally admired are those of rapid, decisive action and 'tough' rather than 'soft' behaviour. The man who makes arrests (even unnecessarily) is thought more admirable than the man of honeyed tongue who resolves all his disputes into 'no cause for police action'.

This, of course, differs slightly from the more idealised picture which came out of our look, earlier, at police dialect. It can perhaps be explained by the fact that the change appears to be comparatively recent. Chief Inspector Hilton's comment provides more evidence of the effect of two developments which will be discussed in a later chapter. One is greater mechanisation as an aid to efficiency, and the other the gap that this creates between police and public, if used unwisely.

As we have seen there is already some gap. A social survey undertaken by the Central Office of Information for the Willink Commission in 1960, suggested:

'There is a further, not inconsiderable disadvantage in police work, and this is the burden of social isolation that the police feel their position carries. This isolation is experienced not only by the police themselves, but to some extent by their wives and children as well. In these respects, police work is probably unique. It follows that the police are continually in a defensive position and any real or imagined criticism from individuals or sections of the general public, the press, or authorities such as the courts or Members of Parliament is liable to produce in the police mind a distorted impression of what the public in general feel about them. There is no way in which the police can assess changes of opinion in their favour, as praise is less likely to be expressed than criticism.'

The police still tend to be over-sensitive and defensive. When they react as if an attack on one is an attack on all, this sense of unity tends to support the prejudice which some of their critics bear against them and who stereotype the police. This gives the impression that all policemen are similar, whereas, within the police, in spite of the tendency towards uniformity that the selection procedure and group discipline encourages, the quality and nature of the individual policeman's response varies. This variation is seldom, however, portrayed to the outside world.

The most persistent and vociferous critics of the police

are black people. No point of friction is potentially more dangerous than with young blacks. The irony is that the reaction of some police and immigrant groups is remarkably similar. When friction does occur, each side tends to stand on its dignity, close ranks and think in stereotypes about the other, expecting the worst of it.

The comment of the 1960 social survey about the police could equally well be applied to black people when it talked of the burden of social isolation that they felt their position carried. Let us continue the quotation, substituting the words 'black men' for 'police'.

'This isolation is experienced not only by black men themselves, but . . . by their wives and children as well. . . . It follows that black men are continually in a defensive position and any real or imagined criticism from individuals or sections of the general public, the press or authorities such as the courts or Members of Parliament, is likely to produce in black men's minds a distorted impression of what the public in general feel about them.'

So perhaps the police are not unique in this respect, as has been stated.

The Mangrove Restaurant incident in London on 9 August 1970 well illustrates the nature of the friction between police and black people. The Mangrove Restaurant was more than its title implied. It had a picture of Malcolm X, the black power leader, on the wall, and, it became clear, was a haven to which black men retreated after meeting prejudice and discrimination in the world outside. Typed leaflets available before a protest march left the restaurant described three police 'raids' on it, though the police themselves have since said they saw no reason why visits should not have been made to see that the law was enforced. Black people, however, saw these visits as an invasion of their territory, of a place they thought they could call their own. They were sensitive

about alleged 'police harassment', though police regarded
the visits as the carrying out of their duty.

It later became apparent, after an opportunity of speaking to policemen in the area, that the police were in a
situation which mirrored that of the blacks. Both sides are
subjected to stereotyping – black people by the colour of
their faces and policemen by their uniforms. Both sides
are subjected to prejudice and scapegoating. The blacks
are thought to be alike and as bad as one another, and
they are blamed by some of the public for the perpetua-
tion of the housing shortage and the shocking conditions
in which many have to live, whereas, in fact, they are
victims. Similarly, policemen are thought by not a few
black people to be alike and as bad as each other. As the
only visible representatives of 'authority' on duty twenty-
four hours a day in the run-down inner city, the policeman is likely to be associated with the neglect of an area
by that authority.

Just like the blacks, the police feel their dignity to be
impaired if insults are hurled at them. A young black,
feeling that he was being picked upon, would retreat to
the Mangrove for solace amongst those whom he could regard as his tribal elders (as one put it to me), and the
feeling of solidarity that comradeship in the face of afflic-
tion can bring. The police equivalent of the Mangrove is
the canteen. Imagine a young policeman on patrol late
at night. There is no lonelier job. He is the only representative in sight of *authority* – authority that has griev-
ously neglected the area, with its shockingly decayed
housing. What is more natural than for him to return to
his 'tribe', as the senior policeman at Bramshill called it,
to a 'cuppa' in the canteen, to seek solace among his mates
after, perhaps, being treated with less dignity than he
thinks he deserved. There are 'tribal elders' in the police,
'George Dixon' type figures ready to help bolster a young
man's confidence, just as black people had their equivalent
at the Mangrove, their 'territory'.

Ironically, the black people chose the local police stations – police territory – as the target for their demonstration, which was about a threat to their territory, the Mangrove. And each of those police stations had its equivalent of the Mangrove – the police canteen. The march moved off from the Mangrove under a banner saying: 'Black Panther Movement . . . Black oppressed people all over the world are one,' and passed the police stations at Notting Hill and Notting Dale with shaken fists and shouted slogans. At the front were the coloured people – perhaps 100 or more – headed by a youth carrying a pig's head. Behind trailed white people, some carrying banners. Suddenly, without warning, in Portnall Road, Paddington, an incident developed a few ranks from the front between one or two demonstrators and police. Within seconds, there were a series of scuffles between police and black men.

The clash brought to a head debate about the attitude of the police as well as the position of the blacks. Since then, police have done much in an attempt to reduce tension in the area, though the real remedy for maintaining public tranquillity lies out of their hands.

It lies with local councillors, social workers, employment officers, educationalists, employers, and central government, to try and ensure that the sense of deprivation that wounds egos and makes some black people into second-class citizens is removed. The police can – and do – make efforts to maintain good relations with the public, and have appointed officers with the specific task of encouraging this. But one thing should not be forgotten. The police, by their nature, are conservative. They must also remain in touch with the slowly moving centre of gravity of society to be able to do their job. They are, by and large, the best of the average men, though containing outstanding officers within their ranks. They have strong Victorian traditions, although they are embracing change, and those traditions spring from a time in which Britain's place in the world and attitude towards 'lesser breeds without the law', as Kipling put it, were different.

Now try and see with those eyes the immense changes that have taken place in society. They have seen the transition from pride in Empire to belief in the Commonwealth; then the gradual erosion of ties as countries in the Commonwealth sought to become republics and have closer links with countries geographically near them; then the turning away from the Commonwealth towards Europe, first to meet rebuff from the French, and then to gain entry. Britain, whose values are represented by the laws which the police enforce and uphold, has ceased to be a world power, but is after all an off-shore island tied to the Continent, whose currency increases in value while ours declines

The presence of the immigrants epitomises the change. It is as if a falling Empire had crashed into Britain's backyard. Moreover, the arrival of the immigrants has been seen by some in the working and lower middle classes, from which most policemen come, to be a threat to the standards those classes have fought to create and preserve.

Great demands are made upon policemen to try and understand the immigrants who may not even speak the same language. Whereas a nod may be as good as a wink to an Englishman, as a policeman exercises his powers of discretion, signals of this sort may not be understood by an immigrant not on quite the same wavelength. Indeed, if a policeman were to nod and wink at some shrewd Asians I know, they might think he was open to a bit of business.

Thus the police are better understood if they are regarded as a sub-group within society, somewhat at a distance from sections of the public, with strong traditions and sensitivity to criticism. If you accept the description by the senior officer at Bramshill of the police as a minority, there is a case for saying that friction between immigrants and police is the problem of a double minority. Though clearly the parallel should not be taken too far, there is another place bedevilled in an obviously more serious way by a double minority problem – Northern Ireland. The strongest safeguard against friction on the police side is the tradition of service to all sections of the community.

The fact is that both the police and black people require a good deal more understanding than has so far been shown. Merely to defend the police and black people – or to attack either – without examining the problems that give rise to the criticism, is dangerously superficial. Symptoms can be mistaken for causes which does neither side any good. It merely leaves each slightly baffled, annoyed and more than a little self-righteous.

5 Practical Coppers

*The policeman suffers from community change –
how prostitutes 'police' each other – a village policeman
exercises his discretion – the dangerous shortage of
Metropolitan Policemen – why officers leave –
crime fighting hindered.*

The coloured people in Britain have acted like a colouring agent used for an X-ray. They show where weaknesses already exist in the body politic. One such weakness is the gap that had already grown between police and sections of the public – a gap which has to be examined from the policeman's point of view also.

The gap between police and public has been exacerbated by increasing urbanisation and by the migration of people within Britain itself, as a result of jobs shake-out and re-training, as Britain's industry becomes more technologically advanced. People moving from old-established communities to new areas become strangers to each other and sometimes to themselves in an increasingly rootless society.

Within cities, redevelopment has torn down those old, well-established communities. In many places, even in cities, they have been quite village-like with their small schools, corner shops and public houses at the centre of local life. People knew each other there. In Liverpool, for instance, the shop was more than a place selling goods. It was, among other things, a meeting place for gossip and advice. Information is no longer circulating in the same way, and the police suffer.

Today, however, the corner shops find it difficult to compete with the more impersonal supermarket, geared to efficiency and large turnover, where instead of gossip, there may be piped music. The pubs may remain, though there are fewer of them, and the old 'home-from-home' has sometimes been tarted up with juke-boxes, even – some of them – with lunch-time topless dancers. People have been uprooted from those communities and put into distant, more anonymous housing schemes. The police find it difficult, if not impossible, to know as many members of the public as individuals in anonymous housing estates and sprawling suburbs.

When asked if the police were allowed to patrol blocks of council flats and, if not, how they kept an eye on them, Scotland Yard said: 'Broadly speaking, police do not regularly patrol areas which are private property and not used by the public in general, but the whole subject of police patrols on council estates is presently under review.' Similar difficulties are posed by large new shopping precincts. One experienced policeman added with a wink, however, that, in case of difficulty, it was always possible to 'receive a request to investigate'.

The diminution of personal contact makes policing more difficult. Mr James Starritt, Deputy Commissioner of the Metropolitan Police, knows its value.

'An old lady who lives in a single room off the Edgware Road may complain that youths go past at 1.0 a.m. and shout, bang doors and knock over her milk bottle and that, because she is old, she cannot get back to sleep again. Being able to talk to a policeman is her idea of him. If he comes along and stops it happening, he has gained a friend and, eventually, she might say one day, when seeing him, "That man over the road has had two new cars in a year," which might start him thinking.'

If the old lady lived in a tall block of flats and her milk bottles had been knocked over, she would not have policemen patrolling on the eighth floot past her door, giving her reassurance, nor would she know very much about the man on the floor below and how many cars he had had, because they would be parked out of sight, down below, and in any case she might see him only in the lift.

In the old part of a Northern city, known for its toughness, the police still maintain a close relationship with the people, whether good or not so good. I went with one policeman at night to a back street pub. He greeted a prostitute, sitting by herself. He explained:

'This is their leisure hour. They don't pick up people here. The licensee wouldn't allow it. They go round the clubs later on. The girls don't want trouble. A group living in one house didn't take men there, because they didn't want it used as a brothel. But one girl always went wild when she had had a few drinks, and also took men back to the house. So the other girls pretended they would all move to London to work, got the girl drunk, put her on the train with a one-way ticket and got off again just before the train left, leaving her aboard. They haven't seen her since. Another prostitute who didn't abide by the pro's code of conduct found that she couldn't get business. Her friends had put it about that she had V.D. Coppers who are not wet behind the ears know how to leave well alone.'

Thus, even prostitutes may self-police themselves, if the policemen who know what is going on allow them to. Getting to know people depends upon trust and the exercise of discretion – once you know the rules of the game that is being played. The northern policeman also said: 'We and the villains understand each other. Villains divide the world into those who "know" and those who "don't know". Policemen, taxi-drivers, prison officers and pub-keepers "know". Social workers, probation officers, vicars and the like "don't know".'

Every police force has its story of how crimes have been solved by the local knowledge possessed by policemen. Just as important, it is by local knowledge that policemen can exercise discretion. The value of this knowledge should never be under-estimated. The following story, which illustrates this, is related by a local policeman in his own words about a missing girl:

'She had been grammar school-educated and came from a good home. Her father was a professional man. She suddenly left home and we treated her as a missing person. Her description was circulated, and eventually someone I knew told me that they had seen her in a local café. I spoke to her and took her to the police station. As she was only just 17, I wanted to know – like all policemen would – what she had been up to. I knew she was associating with a boy who was a bad lot. His mother had been consorting with American servicemen during the war, and he was a product of that. I didn't know to what extent the girl's association with this boy had gone. I got two facts from her. One was that she had taken some money from her grandmother's house a few days previously. That had not been reported. Secondly, even when she was still at school she had been sleeping with this lad. Yet she was friendly also with another boy. You couldn't at this stage call him a boyfriend, but he also came from a good family.

'The two families were quite close, and the son of the second family and she were quite obviously being thrown together. But she had been having it off with this other boy, and it had quite obviously been a regular thing for some time. She had developed a passion for him, and while on the run had been sleeping in his car. I knew there would be a matter of prosecuting him for having carnal knowledge of a girl under 16 – this had all started that long before. But being a village bobby at the time, I had to consider what impact that would have on her and her family. She was very distressed about what had happened. Although that type of discretion should not really be exercised, in the nature of things I thought that I, as the local bobby, knowing these particular circumstances and the effect of them in the village, this sort of thing would have become the subject of gossip and the family would have had to move away.

'I gave her a good talking to, and told her never to mention a word of it to anybody. I then told her family I had found her. I told the boy involved that he could be done for all sorts of things. I warned him that if he ever breathed a word of what happened I would be down on him from a great height. I wonder how many members of the public would realise that I could have been in serious trouble, if I had been found out, for not acting. There is a difference between the case hunter and a policeman who is in the community and thinks of the repercussions of the actions he should be obliged by law to take. I have no time for the case hunter. He uses the word "duty" as a shield. But what is your duty to this young girl and her family? I was a constable. I daren't tell my sergeant. He was a case hunter and lived in a village twelve miles away.

'There is another side to this. This was a village where everyone knew everyone else. I had been there five years. People knew me and my wife. If I had taken the action I was supposed to take under the law, one stands to be judged by the village. "Why bring all this trouble?" they would have said. "Why can't he sort it out?" If it had come to the ears of my superiors, I would have been judged by a policeman who runs a four-minute mile, perhaps, and helps old ladies over the road. That is the level they judge you by. What happened to the girl? In the way of schoolgirl crushes, she got over it. She got married to the other boy who came of the good family.'

It is worth emphasising the main points of the story. The only people in the know were the policeman, the girl and the boy who enticed her away. Her family still do not know the true story. The result was that the girl married someone whom the policeman thought she could spend her life with, and the family was not threatened. The policeman was operating in a situation he could understand, in which he considered he knew what a 'decent' family was, and in which he could separate 'good' from 'bad'. He also knew how the community worked and how it would judge the situation, and what the effect would be. He thought it better that the whole truth should not come out, but he told no lies. This kind of police work, which goes against the book, cannot be taught on courses. Nor do a couple of 'A' levels help. Policemen will tell you that it requires human understanding, wisdom, judgement, tact and a certain amount of courage. No lecturer at a training college would dare to teach a young constable to connive against his superiors in not enforcing the law when, according to all the rules, it should be enforced.

(It is fair to add that there is another interpretation of the event, which might not, however, appeal much to parents of teenage daughters. Critics might think the policeman's views out of keeping with the permissive age, which some policemen do not like – another example of the way a group with Victorian-based traditions clings on to values which, though admirable, are not universally shared.)

It is the ability to make one's own judgements and stand on one's own feet that distinguishes a practical copper from those that are 'wet behind the ears'. But the erosion of communities and the blurring of what is, and is not, morally acceptable, has removed guide lines within which policemen can make judgements and act as this one did. Some people would question whether the officer should have acted as he did. Even the worth of the family is being questioned by some advanced thinkers. The police cling on to safer and narrower moral standards, that had their basis in Victorian times, and this again sets them apart, though not from the silent majority.

The extent to which local knowledge has been prized by the police was illustrated by one officer from another southern force who said that there was a mine of local information contained in beat books, kept by the local bobby to ensure continuity of knowledge. A beat book described the area in which he worked. A policeman newly arriving in the area could see described in the book the important components of life there. It described people who visited once a year, he said, where telephone kiosks were, gave details of hawkers and gypsies, and the families they were connected with, special constables, people who would volunteer to help in times of need, the types of farm and the stock held. There was a section dealing with all the crime that had been committed. He knew of beat books going back to 1840.

'Ninety per cent of the people were on the side of the local bobby,' another country policeman commented. 'He really was a civilian in uniform. He knew them all personally. He was looked on as God. My chief said that the village bobby and sergeant were looked on as the Chief Constables of the area they served. You had the "Ways and Means Act" where the bobby closed his eyes to some things that the Vicar was best able to sort out.'

Today, he went on, there had been a decline in the moral standards established in Victorian times. Communities had been eroded by depopulation. Instead, the villages were being used as dormitories by people who were very conscious of what they regarded as 'their rights'. The spirit of give and take had gone, and numbers of police were seen to be inadequate. So the police had done what the military would. In his Force they had withdrawn to strategic areas. They had stripped the country areas of policemen and concentrated them in urban centres, from which they went to the country areas by vehicle. There was an outcry from the local people. They did not have a local policeman to identify with. Instead, they had a man going through the area once a week. Ninety per cent of policing thus disappeared, he said. 'We took away the man who was doing preventive policing. Now you get coming in some sharp little detective from training school, who can't identify with the local people.'

The gap between police and public has always been greater in the more anonymous city, but it is increased by the fact that policemen seldom live among the people they serve. It is quite common for officers to commute a distance to work. One Metropolitan Police Inspector commented ruefully: 'We move into areas daily like an occupying force.' Anyway, policemen do not wish to live with their families in areas with some of the most intractable social problems. Older policemen want to buy their houses outside central London. Young recruits are found accommodation in police section houses.

Anthony Judge, editor of the Police Federation's monthly magazine *Police*, says in his book *A Man Apart*: 'In London, nearly every young policeman lives in a police section house. These are distributed over the Metropolitan Police area, and one advantage to the Force is that they provide large concentrations of men who can, if the need arises, be called out immediately.'

This no doubt also contributes to some extent to the insulation of police in the areas in which they work, although policemen, and young officers especially, are encouraged to participate in voluntary work, particularly among youth. The police are already put at some distance from the public by the nature of their work.

There is, as well, another insidious factor at work – the shortage of policemen in certain key areas, inner London among them. This is another important reason for the gap between police and public. The Police Federation has been warning about the dangers for some years, particularly of the wastage from the police of experienced constables – the backbone of the Force. That continuing concern was expressed at the Federation's 1973 annual conference at Blackpool, when a resolution was passed calling for a government inquiry into establishments. Reorganisation of the police boundaries is also blamed for the lowering of morale that causes premature retirements and hinders recruiting.

In spite of this concern, however, Mr Robert Carr, the Home Secretary, was able to tell the 1973 Federation conference that the net gain in police strength in England and Wales in 1972 was about 3,000. This compared with a net gain of only about 1,000 in 1969, and, at the end of April, he said, there were 100,000 police officers, 6,500 traffic wardens and 29,500 civilians in the police service in England and Wales.

Compared with three years before, he said, that represented a net increase of 6,800 police officers, 2,000 traffic wardens and nearly 5,000 civilians. 'I am anxious that the drive for more policemen and more people to release policemen for operational duties should continue.' But Mr Carr admitted: 'I am seriously concerned about the manpower situation in the Metropolitan Police which had a net loss in strength in 1972 and in the first months of this year. The really worrying problem here is not so much recruitment, which has been rather better than in the provinces, but wastage.'

Earlier, Mr Reginald Gale, then the Federation's Chairman, had told the conference that, in less than five months in 1973, the Metropolitan Force had lost 203 of its strength. And Mr G. Rowland, an Inspector from Northwood, in the Metropolitan Force, said it was not only losing men at an unprecedented rate each week. He added: 'We already have sufficient vacancies to absorb the whole of the Bedfordshire and Luton Force, plus Dorset and Bournemouth, plus Gwynned or Dyfed-Powys, plus mid-Anglia and Suffolk and would still have sufficient vacancies left to take in every single delegate in this hall today.'

Though the Federation has always been wedded to a national rate of pay, it changed its policy and decided, against opposition, to seek, after the second stage of the government's counter-inflation policy, a non-pensionable allowance for the officers in the Metropolitan Force up to the rank of Chief Inspector.

Yet pay was given by only two out of 557 people as a reason for leaving the Metropolitan Force in the twelve months up to December 1972. Seventeen went to join police forces overseas, 54 gave hours, shifts and duties as reasons for leaving, 98 gave domestic reasons, 47 were emigrating, 130 said that they were unsuitable for police work, 184 took other employment, and 25 gave miscellaneous reasons. Expert opinion is that a wife today has more say in the kind of work her husband does. She wants an adequate life of her own. On the other hand, the *mystique* of the police force has disappeared, though it still remains for most a vocation.

Two policemen have given separately their reasons for leaving the Force in greater detail. Both, by coincidence, were emigrating to New Zealand, and one said that at his station half a dozen officers were interested in going, but could not for family reasons. Both officers laid great stress on the decline in educational standards in London, and wanted their children to go to better schools. Both emphasised the strain of doing long hours of duty, and one said he would be happy with his income if he could have more hours off, though with more money he could afford a more suitable house. Both spoke of the strain of having to go to court next day after duty the previous night. 'You could work all night here, finish at 6–7 in the morning, and then you have to be in court at 10 o'clock.'

Both officers spoke of the disruption of family life because of unexpected duties, which meant social engagements had to be cancelled.

There was also a conflict between what the regulations said should not be done, and what policemen were expected to do to enforce the law. They had to get round them. One of the officers, P.C. Curd said:

'We have a power under the Metropolitan Police Act which authorises us to stop and search people in the street, if they are acting suspiciously, or we have reason to believe that they have stolen property. If you were a trained policeman you might be able to spot one every two months. But we do stop people every day and we do get a lot of success. But if you stop people, you are taking a chance. You don't know most times. . . . You are expected quite rightly to do stops, whereas in fact you haven't the reason, according to the regulations.'

The second officer said:

'I think the basic reason why people join the police, ambulance services and so on is a basic love of humanity. Once you join, particularly the police, you are shot at from all sides, criticising you doing this and that – from inside the job, from the public, and from all sides. You are not ostensibly backed by anybody. Nobody says: "Well done". Well, if they do, it is on odd occasions. When I used to go anywhere I used to be quite proud of being a policeman. Being a policeman now is the last thing I will admit to people. People disappear into the corner of the room and won't speak to me.'

In fact, all the problems are interrelated. Mr Peter Joiner, secretary of the Metropolitan branch of the Police Federation, says that pay is a contributory factor – among others.

'It is very often the last straw that breaks the camel's back. He (the policeman) might be under tremendous pressure from his wife about hours of work and not being able to have holidays when he wants them. He might not be able to have Saturday off, because he has to go and police a football match. So he doesn't get the car washed. In the end, he says: "I will get a job with a five-day week, even if I lose two pounds a week." That does not mean, however, that pay is not a factor. If you dangle a sufficiently large carrot you will get large numbers of men coming forward. You can get better applicants. People would stay longer. And this would enable you to improve conditions all round. If you had more men available, you would give people more days off and you would have to cancel leaves less frequently. You would not have to use the same men on Saturdays for football matches and at other times for "demos" over and over again, having them stand by, when they may or may not be needed. If the "demos" do not happen, you still have to have men on duty waiting.'

The pressures also reflect the response of the policeman to his duties. Policemen must, like people in other jobs, face the annual onslaught of camera-clicking, rubber-necking tourists. But few in the tourist trade are quite so exposed as the policeman. Mr Joiner went on: 'Every one of them is entitled to ask questions from the police officer. He is confronted with a constant barrage of questions. Another policeman may find that he is on continual patrol in one of the less salubrious parts of London.' Pressures were so great he would have to decide which part of his work to do. In Soho the law was being broken all the time. The policeman had to decide what service to give the public because, if he pursued all the law-breakers in Soho, he would be off the street for a good deal of the time.

Mr Starritt, Deputy Commissioner of the Metropolitan Police said:

'You get complaints that policemen are not as considerate as they used to be. It is partly to do with the pressures, perhaps from shortage of men. It is probably the brashness of youth, anyway. We should not forget that the public are more demanding and all of us are under more pressure. One is constantly talking about this and stressing how important it is. The best men always appear to have time. One of the problems of the young – and there are a lot of young policemen – is that they have not always got the time. It is also a matter of confidence. Sadly, like most other organisations, we are not always able to confer the talent with the appointment.'

Mr Starritt added:

'In some places, under the traditional form of policing, we do not have manpower to fill all the beats. . . . People do not see a policeman as often as they used to. It is not generally realised that the uniformed police are dealing with almost 60 per cent of crime reported. They had to do this because, through shortage of manpower, crimes were not being investigated as thoroughly as we would wish.'

One of the places under pressure was Kentish Town, North London, where Chief Superintendent W. Burrows was struggling, in December 1972, to cover his area from a gaunt old police station due to be replaced in 1975. The pride the men have in the old 'nick' is reflected in the care taken over the front garden. Kentish Town is divided into six 'home beats' with two Panda cars superimposed on them. The six 'home beat' men were doing an eight-hour day. But, with the Pandas, there was twenty-four-hour cover. There were also six men on street patrols.
Mr Burrows said:

'The ideal would be ten beats, but you would need fifty men to work a twenty-four-hour coverage. Superimposed on that you would need men to walk the patrols in busy areas. (You need five men to each beat to fill it for twenty-four-hours.) And you would need another forty men for foot patrols. But instead of that ideal we have five home beats covering twice as big an area as the old beat in the old system. . . . Because of shortage of men, some parts are not policed regularly by foot, but cars are used instead. If you went back to the pre-war situation, you would have thirty beats in Kentish Town. But today, there will always be at some part of the twenty-four hours a home beat man patrolling his beat. If I had another forty men on my present strength of ninety-two, I could cover the ground with men on foot. I cannot do that at the moment. There are places which rarely see an officer on foot. We usually have eight men, besides the home beat men, available on a Saturday night, plus two Panda cars and one area wireless car. If we have six doing duty when trouble breaks out at two places our strength has to be divided. We can send three to one area and three to another. But the other areas on the ground are unpoliced, except for the cars, though we have as well the home beat officers. Broadly, our home beat men look after the static population, and the rest are looked after by other officers. We have been down to five men available from the station.'

Commander Peter Marshall, who was then in command of 'E' Division, of which Kentish Town is part, added:

'You are also stretched by the calls made on you from demonstrations elsewhere. You may be down to an availability of five men or less. The result is that back streets have little contact with policemen. But the work produced by fewer policemen is higher. Our crime arrest figure is up this year (1972) over last. The same number of men have dealt with more allegations.'

The crippling shortage of men was also hampering work in West End Central, which covers the heart of London – Mayfair, Soho, Leicester Square, and the area round the Strand and Covent Garden. There were 681 uniformed officers in December 1972 as against an establishment of 852, and twenty-eight policewomen out of an establishment of thirty-two. This meant that the uniformed police were about 20 per cent under strength. Many had to work overtime, and their weekends had to be interrupted to cover demonstrations. The area includes such places needing cover as the U.S. Embassy, Ulster Office, South Africa House, India House, the Greek Embassy, Indonesian Embassy and the Embassy of the United Arab Republic.

Commander David Helm, who was in charge of the Division thought that a lot of the policemen there, who included a high proportion of young constables, felt that they could earn better pay outside with less restrictions on their private life.

'He is a policeman twenty-four hours a day. Always he has to bear in mind he is a policeman. Should anything happen, he might be called upon to act as a policeman. If he is doing anything that brings discredit upon the service, he is subject to the discipline code. One of the things they say is a restriction is that we are still trying to keep hair at a reasonable length. They say that earmarks them as policemen at dances and so on. And they are missing out on modern trends. A lot of the lads live in the Section House in the middle of Soho. Although quarters are reasonable, they leave a lot to be desired, if they are not used to living away from home. Another annoying source of wastage is to other Forces, where they can buy property at reasonable prices. Property in London is out of the reach of the majority of P.C.s. Also, I understand, some Forces do give help in buying property. A reasonable house near enough for a man to travel into work in London would cost £12,000.'

Because of the shortage of uniformed men the pressure on each was increased, Commander Helm added. Because of leaves and shifts there were roughly 100 available for each relief. Out of those, men had to be posted to guard embassies, to cover demonstrations – which sometimes came up quickly – and to help clear traffic jams. (There are fifty-one miles of roads in the Division and the peak-hour traffic flow at Piccadilly Circus is 6,000 vehicles an hour.) When all the duties were taken into account, he was down to no more than fifty men in a division which had a rateable value of £14½ million. He added:

'We need more men to enforce the law as we would like to. We have to create a balance in enforcing the law. We know that our main target is crime. Vice is a problem, traffic is a problem, street traders are a problem. We have to create a balance between all this and the men we have. Take pornography. If I had fifty men to do nothing else but that, I might not clear it up completely, but I would make it very hard to trade.

'You have to sort out your order of priorities. In a month, we have had two murders. Men have to be drafted in to help, but they have to come from somewhere. The police can give only a certain amount of time to certain crime. There will come a time when we will say that, if we have the evidence, we will investigate it, but if we have not, we will just have to be content with recording it in the hope that we can open up an investigation later if something turns up to give us a lead.'

Although the 104 CID men and four CID women in the Division were up to strength at the time, Det. Chief Supt. A. W. Lampard said: 'If we had more men, the clear-up rate would be better. Some crimes which look absolutely hopeless we have to leave. We have to concentrate on those we can solve.'

It became apparent on listening to hard-pressed officers, struggling without adequate manpower to fight increasingly vicious crime, that the Force was under such pressure that the safety of London was being endangered. It is not the fault of the police. Their dedication in the face of tremendous obstacles remains impressive. But it is beyond their power to tackle all crime properly and, with the steady, reassuring presence of the police too often absent, the gap between public and police is increased.

Already, as we have seen, environmental change, insecurity and rehousing are eroding the subtle relationship between police and public. The nature of the policeman's work already isolates him to some extent, and that isolation is being increased. Although radio links the policeman with his colleagues he is in other ways becoming a more lonely figure. Stories are told bitterly by some policemen how, when they have been attacked, the public have stood by watching, without giving aid.

There is a danger that the public will look on the police simply as doing a dirty job for them, of which they want no part. Unless current trends are reversed, there is also a danger that by the destruction of communities the public's ability to induce good behaviour out of respect for others will be reduced. If people no longer 'self-police', this could mean a radical and unwelcome change in the nature of police work. And this, like the real causes of public tranquillity or the prevention of crime, would be beyond the police, in the final analysis, to prevent.

6 A Crisis of Confidence

The pressures on erring policemen – leadership at the Yard – Sir Robert Mark and controversy – changes in the Metropolitan Police – dealing with policemen in trouble.

When shortage of men – with the resulting long hours demanded of individuals – is combined with a sense of overriding 'tribal' loyalty, a situation is created in which short cuts may be taken and officers cover up for each other so that faults can remain hidden. Sometimes this can happen to a dangerous extent if senior officers do not exercise sufficiently strict control.

An inquiry into the rhinoceros whip affair at Sheffield, conducted by a QC and an Inspector of Constabulary, said:

'The minds of the appellants were already conditioned by the dangerous notion they had formed that a Crime Squad was a *corps d'élite* which could use tough methods to deal with tough criminals and take risks to achieve speedy results. . . . Mr ――― . . . told us that he held views that criminals are treated far too softly by the courts, that because criminals break rules, police may and must do so to be a jump ahead.'

The Sheffield Force had not increased its establishment since 1947, its CID was reduced in size between 1953 and 1958, while crime increased by 25 per cent. Its fifty detectives in 1962 worked more than 16,000 hours of unpaid overtime for which they could not be compensated by time off in lieu.

The inquiry found that the mitigation for the two

detective constables who carried out 'deliberate, unprovoked, brutal and sustained assaults, with weapons in the nature of a truncheon and a short flexible piece of gut-like material, upon prisoners who were defenceless and did not retaliate, for the purpose of inducing confessions of crime', was:

(a) they had been working long hours and were over-tired and hungry;
(b) they were, and felt, under pressure to obtain results;
(c) their use of violence had been encouraged by hints beforehand, and it had been instituted and witnessed with approval by senior officers;
(d) that these senior officers and another detective constable who joined in the violence were wholly inadequately dealt with by the Chief Constable;
(e) that they had been told to give a false account in court by a senior officer, who concocted it.

Since then, the Sheffield Force has been restored to high reputation. Members of the Select Committee on Race Relations and Immigration were struck by the good relations with the coloured communities in the city, and the enlightened efforts made to achieve them. The Sheffield Affair was exceptional, and no one is suggesting that anything like a similar situation existed in the Metropolitan Police, but it would be unwise to forget its lessons about the effect of pressure on men.

As long ago as 1929, a Royal Commission on the Police reported:

'Some of the CID (Scotland Yard) evidence which we have heard leaves a disquieting impression on our minds. There is, we fear, a tendency among this branch of the service to regard itself as a thing above and apart, to which the restrictions and limitations placed upon the ordinary police do not, or should not, apply. This error, if not checked, is bound to lead to abuses which may grow until they bring discredit upon the whole Force.'

The forecast came tragically true with the exposure by *The Times* in 1969 of 'an unhappy story written with legal advice and without pleasure. It is an account of corruption, greed, cynicism and injustice', *The Times* continued. As a result of the story of corruption, two detectives went to gaol. A third detective failed to surrender to his bail to answer seven charges of corruption. The two reporters who did the investigation, Julian Mounter and Gareth Lloyd, were later said by Lord Justice Edmund Davies in the Court of Appeal in respect of the two jailed detectives to have 'rendered a great public service'. He added: 'It was, it would appear, mainly their intrepidity and skill which laid bare a hideous cancer which, if unchecked, could have done even greater and incalculable damage to law enforcement. It accordingly seems to us only right that we should pay them tribute, and that we now do.'

Yet there are some policemen who are still prepared to say that their colleagues were treated unfairly by *The Times*. One of a group of officers from another Force three years later felt that the police service had been attacked by outsiders and its authority undermined. He was, however, rebuked by a colleague who pointed out that the officer would surely not wish to leave the impression that he was condoning offences by the two detectives. The police, he said, were not above the law.

The Times' disclosures focused unprecedented attention on the Metropolitan Police and were eventually followed by the most radical policy changes the Force had experienced in years. Those changes were introduced by Sir Robert Mark, who took over as Metropolitan Police Commissioner in 1972 from Sir John Waldron. Sir John was a policeman of the old school, straightforward, rather stiff, but kindly, transparently honest and loyal to his men. Mr Peter Brodie, the Assistant Commissioner in charge of the

CID was also much liked by his men. He remembered details of their families, such as the number of children they had, one told me.

He studied their interests, and under him CID men felt that they had status. If Mr Brodie and Sir John had a fault, they were too trusting. They expected to be treated with the loyalty they gave to their men. But that sort of world, in which leadership had an old-fashioned gentlemanly quality about it – not to be disparaged – had changed. Sir John and Mr Brodie were good men, poorly repaid. Moreover there was a tendency for the CID to regard itself as an elite. It had become a force within a force, as the 1929 Royal Commission on the Police had feared it would, long before Mr Brodie became head of the CID.

The crisis of confidence which faced the Metropolitan Police after *The Times* case focused on to the question of the leadership of the Force. Sir John had reached the age of retirement. Who would follow him? Though never officially acknowledged, there was a battle for power going on between Mr Brodie and Mr Robert Mark, the Deputy Commissioner, as he then was. Though still veiled, the issue became a public one after two senior detectives gave an interview to *The Times* in 1971. Their identity has never been disclosed by the newspaper. But in a speech to the Monday Club, the right-wing Conservative organisation, in 1972 after the leadership issue had been settled in favour of Mr Mark, Mr Brodie said:

'I saw some very senior people of *The Times* newspaper. I did this with the consent of my Commissioner. I gave them my ideas. I woke up to find a front page article which left no doubt at all that they were referring to me. They had produced an article which was tantamount to saying that Peter Brodie was against the Establishment. You can imagine the effect it had on the Home Office. It didn't do me any good.'

The Times interview began:

'In a rare and remarkable statement of police philosophy senior officers at Scotland Yard have angrily condemned Parliament, the courts and the Home Office for being persistently lenient in their treatment of people convicted of crimes of violence.

'Alarmed by the rapid increase of these crimes, the officers are convinced that unless firm measures are taken to halt the trend, the streets of London will be as dangerous in five years time as those of New York and Washington now.

'Exasperated by what they consider to be a lack of government support, the officers, in an exclusive interview with *The Times* talked bitterly of the disproportionate publicity given to the views of "Do-gooders". They said that was the reason why they had decided to speak out.

' "Organisations such as the National Council for Civil Liberties are a vociferous minority," one of them told me. "They do all the thumping and get all the publicity. The majority, the other 98 per cent, are silent, but we believe we have their support.

' "The trouble is that we can't climb on a soap box at Marble Arch on a Sunday afternoon and say so. We also know that no government will change its policy and risk losing votes, unless it is pushed by public opinion. . . ." '

The senior officer who did most of the talking said: 'Of course, I admire the rehabilitation efforts of successive governments. I do not wish to be harsh on the chap for whom there may be some ray of hope.'

But he added:

' "If we want to stop crime escalating somebody has got to put his foot down very, very firmly. We want no more parole or suspended sentences for men convicted of crimes of violence. There must be penal establishments for them where there will be more discipline, more work, where

they will perform tasks in their cells and there will be no
television, no radio, no choice of food, no weekend leave." '

This hard-line approach echoes what a lot of policemen
feel, and not only in London. Their favourite complaints
are against the naivety of social workers and sloppy senti-
mentality of penal reforms.

What made the interview with the two Yard detectives
even more pertinent was that, only four days before, a lecture given by Mr Mark to the Police College, Bramshill,
had also been given prominence in *The Times*. His rather
different approach stood out, in contrast, the clearer. He
agreed that in many sophisticated societies violence arising
from crime was regarded as one of the more serious current problems. But he went on:

'The understandable doubts and misgivings provoked by
what is loosely called "the permissive society" and emo-
tional reaction to reports of criminal violence – murder,
sexual and other assaults, robbery and burglary – tend to
obscure the less newsworthy but happier aspects of inevitable social change. A society which has begun to regard
life as more valuable than property has surely made progress?'

That small paragraph alone is worth examining for
what it tells about the man. He does not like loose thinking, or over-emotional reactions, and thinks that people
should look beyond the headlines to what is really happening and view it within a somewhat broader perspective.

His lecture continued:

'Though there are still manifest inequalities, it can hardly
be disputed that there is less poverty, that more people
have greater opportunities, that social issues evoke a wider
response. The growing realisation that there are objectives
for criminal justice more important and constructive than
mere punishment is surely an indication of change for the
better?'

Mr Mark also showed himself to be in tune with government policy. And like all good policemen, whether they stop you in the street as a suspected person or are lecturing at the Police College, he is able to reason: the bad policeman merely asserts. Mr Mark's lecture went on:

'Successive governments since the last war have without exception wisely been inclined to favour a cautious and gradual approach to the various remedies for the increase in crime.

'There has been, as well, an attempt to bring the law more up to date and in keeping with contemporary thought and to achieve, so far as is proper, a greater uniformity in enforcement of the more common offences. But there has been no attempt to increase police resources beyond the minimum thought appropriate to maintain a reasonable degree of public confidence. And most significantly there has been no attempt to achieve greater effectiveness by increasing the powers of the police under the law.'

The fascination of the two approaches – that of the two detectives and Mr Mark – lies in the contrast of their philosophies and style. That of the two detectives is direct, forthright, aggressive. Mr Mark's is more of a reconnaissance of the problems facing the police, before deciding what his next moves shall be, although, if the text is scrutinised carefully, there are hints of policies he was to urge later, as his thinking evolved.

But Mr Mark, as Deputy Commissioner, could not at that stage be explicit about them. The result was a misunderstanding of his true nature. He was wrongly regarded as being soft towards traditional enemies of the police. This was partly because he was in favour of the abolition of hanging. This was not simply because of his views about capital punishment *per se*. It was a component in a much wider argument, which he has since deployed with great force. He reasoned that, if hanging were abolished, it would be possible to alter the emphasis of the law, which was balanced, in his view, too much in favour of the criminal.

Just as in dealing with traffic problems or public turbulence the police cannot be effective by themselves (they are not operating in a vacuum), so they need support in curbing serious crime. As long ago as 1966 Mr Mark was maintaining that they could not do it alone. He then wrote in the *Criminal Law Review*:

'It cannot be said that the criminal law today is even reasonably effective. Even worse, it actually appears to be unfair. The great majority of weak, simple or incompetent wrongdoers obscures its inadequacy to deal with the professional criminal who enjoys too high a degree of immunity from it. I suggest that in those circumstances it is timely, proper and in the public interest to vary the system of investigation and trial so that the burden of proof can be more easily discharged by the prosecution.'

In the course of his arguments over the next two years, in which he developed this theme, he stated that it was necessary to transform the criminal trial from a show-jumping contest into an inquiry to establish the truth.

Two of the changes he has argued for have come about: majority verdicts in jury trials and the disclosure of alibi defences before trials. He also advocated the requirement for the accused to enter the witness box and the abolition of the forms of caution in the Judges' Rules. As he pointed out:

'The rules are well known. The forms of caution against self-incrimination in the Rules have never been of the slightest use to the innocent. They have been – and still are – of inestimable value to the guilty and have no doubt gladdened the heart of many a lawyer as enhancing the *mystique* of the criminal law in a way conveniently likely to obscure the real issue in a trial.'

It is a powerful and well-rounded argument, seductively favouring the weighing of the scales of justice a little more heavily on one side against the liberal goodies that balance it on the other. In both their strength and weakness, Sir Robert's powers of reasoning are not unlike those of Mr Enoch Powell, though obviously the content of their speeches is different. Their arguments advance on a broad front, from a premise in a logical progression towards a conclusion designed to achieve action. But the logic is sometimes taken further than some would feel justified on the grounds of common sense.

Doubts arose when the Criminal Law Revision Committee came out with a report on 28 June 1972 that supported Sir Robert's arguments. The Committee recommended that the police caution should be abolished and also the right of an accused person to make an unsworn statement. Refusal to give evidence on oath could count as corroboration of evidence against him in appropriate circumstances. There were fears that with such changes safeguards against conviction of the innocent would also disappear.

There were good reasons from the police point of view for advocating that the balance of justice ought to be readjusted a little. Some detectives claim that they sometimes have to cut corners to get the convictions that society demands. They know when a villain is guilty, they insist. So there are pressures to put a bit of gloss on the evidence, they say, not dishonestly, but merely to ensure that the truth comes out. Adjusting the scales of justice would therefore reduce temptations for policemen to cut corners. They could instead rely more on the courts to get at the truth. Critics of this police attitude say that already there are instances of people giving false 'confessions' and being urged to have other crimes taken into account, 'so as to make things easier all round'. In fact, it is claimed, this is a well-tried method of clearing up crime on the police books.

The temptation for policemen to cut corners is increased also by the shortage of manpower. The inquiry into the Sheffield rhino whip affair found that the detectives concerned had been working long hours and were overtired and hungry. They were, and felt, under pressure to achieve results.

Detectives in the Metropolitan Police are under tremendous pressure, though it should not be assumed that all policemen automatically go wrong as a result. It may in fact indicate how well they withstand pressures and do not cut corners, in spite of the tremendous demands society makes upon them and without giving them adequate resources. As in so many other things for which the police are blamed, a lot of the fault lies outside their control and, in the past, they have been inhibited from speaking out. The following figures were compiled in May, 1973: In 'P' Division of the Metropolitan Police each CID officer had an average annual case load of 444·2. The lowest figure is in 'N' Division, with an average of 283 per CID officer each year. A further indication of the variations is that of individual police stations. For instance, Sydenham has an annual case load of 723 per CID officer, whereas West Drayton has the lowest – a minimum of 161 per CID officer.

Another way of looking at the pressure on officers is to examine the hours worked each week by CID officers. Figures are compiled from the 'C' Department operational branches at Scotland Yard from the hours worked of divisional CID officers. The figures quoted indicate a weekly average and experience has shown that this is not subject to much variation, although some CID officers work more hours than those shown:

	Hours
Detective Chief Inspectors and Detective Inspectors	61·62
Detective Sergeants	60·72
Detective Constables	59·70

The effect of this pressure is also to limit the amount of time that can be spent by individual officers on cases and to force the police, against their wishes, to arrange them in some sort of priority. The problem of deciding priorities is not, of course, confined to the Metropolitan Police. Mr Walter Stansfield, Chief Constable of the Force which serves the city and county of Derby, writes in *The Police We Deserve*:

'Just how does one decide priorities? Most people would agree that those committing savage crimes against society – murder, brutal rape, armed robberies – should be pursued relentlessly no matter what public expenditure is involved.... It is hoped thereby that the murderer or author of the major crime will be brought to justice, but in the process lesser crimes that would otherwise have been detected because sufficiently investigated will never be solved and the culprits go free. Other offences that would have been prevented by the presence of a police officer now on other duties will be reported and swell the crime rate.'

Anthony Judge in *A Man Apart* referred to the same problem:

'The police have been turning their attention away from a simple consideration of crime in terms of statistics towards a closer analysis of what the figures mean in terms of social damage to the community. In other words, which crimes are so serious that every effort must be made to prevent and detect them, and which are relatively trivial in the sense that they involved minor thefts where only the loser is the complainant?'

He added that following studies in America the Home Office Police Research and Development Branch was conducting its own examination of the feasibility of a crime-seriousness scale. Mr Judge noted that the English criminal law had traditionally placed heavy emphasis on the sanctity of private property, a situation which in itself placed the police, in the eyes of some sections of the community, as protectors of property and the property owners. It would seem reasonable to suggest, he argued, that nowadays people would place more importance on the role of the police as the protectors of the citizen against violent attack.

Mr Judge said: 'If the police are to concentrate on violence, for example, such crimes as shoplifting and thefts of property from unattended motor cars, which account for a significant proportion of the total crime figures, would have to receive less attention.'

Thus it can be seen that the pressure on the police is affecting not only the way the individual policeman can do his job, but is making it impossible for the police to live fully up to their original objectives. The middle ranks of the police are also suffering. Clearly because a policeman is hard-pressed does not mean that he will unavoidably go bad. Very much depends upon him as an individual and the values he possesses. But for any policeman who finds it difficult to resist the undoubted temptations that could be put in his way – he is, after all, dealing with villains and must be put on trust to a great extent – those temptations are increased if pressure of work on his superiors means that they cannot supervise him to the extent that they would wish.

Sir Robert thus had to take decisive action when he became Commissioner of Police in April, 1972. Mr Colin Woods, the Assistant Commissioner in charge of the traffic department, had already been appointed head of the CID, Mr Brodie having retired. Mr Woods is a quiet man with a wry sense of humour, enigmatic smile and an imaginative probing mind which examines ideas disconcertingly by leaping from viewpoint of them to viewpoint. He has, like many of the new breed of top policemen a managerial expertise, and uses such boardroom jargon as 'husbanding resources', 'quality of manpower' and 'needing to concentrate effort'. He talks also in language that policemen can understand: 'feeling collars' is an example.

Sir Robert had to take command at a time when the morale of the CID was not high. Many of its officers did not much like the ideas which Sir Robert began introducing. His difficult task was to maintain pride in the job while removing the feeling that the CID was a force within a force – the worry of the 1929 Royal Commission. His plan for interchange of staff between CID and the rest of the Force made some detectives feel that they were in danger of being moved willy-nilly into a job with less status. They also complained of the danger of losing detective allowances. Sir Robert's intentions were threefold: to release the full talents of the Force in a unified fight against crime by breaking down artificial barriers between departments; to create greater flexibility; and to allow men career opportunities on a much wider basis.

The old structure had allowed the CID much independence. Its Assistant Commissioner had transmitted policy and directions through, firstly, his deputy assistant commissioner in charge of administration and divisions (the geographical areas into which the Force is divided) and then through CID area commanders, in theory to the uniformed commanders of the divisions. In practice, lines of communication from the CID top men at the Yard had tended to be more direct to CID chief superintendents in divisions.

Handling serious complaints against the police with an allegation of crime had been the responsibility of the Assistant Commissioner in charge of the CID. He had appointed the investigating officer and sent the papers to the Director of Public Prosecutions. The comparative autonomy of the CID had produced from one point of view an *esprit de corps* in which the ability to catch criminals had depended upon close understanding between colleagues and the development of detective skills and techniques as a sort of arcane alchemy. Unfortunately, recent convictions of CID men had led to public and political disquiet.

More than half of those usually suspended had come from the CID, which comprised only 15 per cent of the Force.

As a result of Sir Robert's changes, the four CID area commanders were put to work under the four uniformed deputy assistant commissioners who comprised the inspectorate. The intention is that the CID expertise available to them will enable more detailed scrutiny of the department's affairs. That scrutiny is also being applied to the deployment of uniformed officers. The twenty-three divisional commanders are uniformed men. Sir Robert made sure that they would control all 2,300 detectives in the divisions – that is, two-thirds of all the detectives in the Force. They also assess them for promotion.

Those uniformed commanders themselves come under a uniformed man – the Assistant Commissioner 'A' who is responsible for all men in uniform, other than traffic. Thus, for discipline purposes, the CID men in the divisions would in future not be under the assistant commissioner in charge of the CID. Under Sir Robert the deputy commissioner, who has overall responsibility for discipline, has come much more to the fore. The assistant commissioner in charge of the CID has become much more responsible to the top echelons. To ensure greater unity at the top, Sir Robert has created a 'cabinet' of top-ranking officers. The atmosphere between them is more relaxed than it used to be, although there is no doubt who is in charge.

With the top echelons readjusted, much of the future depends upon the quality of personnel. Some officers have been over-promoted and many have been under-promoted. To be successful, an officer aspiring to the higher levels of the CID must now be more than a good thief-taker. Personal qualities, notably integrity, weigh heavily.

From the men already promoted, it is possible to see some of the qualities that Sir Robert is seeking. Chief Superintendent Peter Marshall was moved rapidly from head of the crime prevention section to the hot-spot of Notting Hill as divisional chief superintendent, and then to be commander of the division covering Camden, a borough which has a lively social conscience, as he himself does – he looks beyond the immediate causes of crime to the nature of the environment which gives rise to it. He has since been put in charge of the community relations section, thus dealing with one of the most sensitive problems facing the Metropolitan Police. Commander David Powis, who has done much in Brixton and Notting Hill to ease relationships between black people and the police and is yet versatile enough to have commanded the Special Patrol Group, a controversial task force of uniformed officers sent to areas requiring intensive policing, has become a deputy assistant commissioner in the inspectorate of the Force. Mr John Alderson, formerly commandant of the Police College, Bramshill, and a policeman of vision and clear ethical standards, was brought in as assistant commissioner in charge of recruiting, training and personnel (he has since been appointed chief constable of Devon and Cornwall). And the key position of Commander, A10, the new department created to handle complaints against the police, has been given to Commander R. H. Anning, who is alert yet has an ease of manner that inspires confidence. He is firm but human, and clearly no Cromwellian. His whole manner, tempered with a quiet good humour, belies early criticism of his branch as 'gestapo'. Such men as these are the best of the British police, and that means the best in the world.

The formation of A10 is a key component in Sir Robert's wider strategy. Commander Anning gives the clue to it when he says: 'Ultimately you retain co-operation from the public only while they have confidence in you. The public would not have confidence in a police force that did not put its own house in order. What other organisation has taken steps like the police, or has expressed willingness to be further accountable by having the findings of complaints independently reviewed afterwards?'

In the three years up to January 1973, 288 Metropolitan

Policemen had been in serious trouble. By far the largest number – eighty in 1972 and 171 over the three years – had been in disciplinary or criminal cases and allowed to retire early. The others had been convicted, were awaiting trial, or had been dismissed or asked to resign. Some of the complaints then being dealt with related to events before Sir Robert became Commissioner. In fact, the figure of 144 officers in serious trouble in 1972 was roughly double those in each of the preceding two years.

The 1972 figure was not a measure of what was then wrong with the Metropolitan Police, but could be regarded as a new determination to bring to justice, either within the Force or before the courts, police officers believed to have done wrong. Such determined and fair investigation is essential to keep public confidence. Because such determination had previously been lacking – through complacency rather than connivance – the reputation of the many excellent officers in the Force suffered.

Not unexpectedly this determination has had a mixed reception. One Metropolitan detective retiring voluntarily as soon as he could said:

'This is not the police force I joined. It is now too dangerous to cut corners. You cannot be a good policeman unless you do. You are getting to the stage today of policemen being frightened by their own shadows. You are in trouble unless you do the bureaucratic paper work. There are not enough people to do the paper work.

'There have always been crooked policemen. Just because you put a helmet on and wear a uniform it does not mean you are pure. This witch-hunt is ridiculous. You cannot do your job for fear of looking over your shoulder.

'Robert Mark is determined to have a lily-white police force. He will have a lily-white police force looking pretty in the street. You cannot have people on the beat with a Bible in one hand and a truncheon in the other. The public pay you to trust you. The trouble with this job is that there are more chiefs than Indians.'

When Mr Brodie talked to the Monday Club after retiring from command of the CID, he referred to the number of complaints. They were the biggest bugbear, he
said. Usually they were unfounded.

'Men are getting fed-up with these allegations. They
don't gain anything from making an arrest. When a complaint is made you get an inquiry set up. Everyone gets so
excited. This is what breaks policemen's hearts – criminals
know that attack is the best means of defence. A policeman
goes in and he stirs up a bee-hive. Then the complaints
come in and they can prejudice an officer's career. If we
can we have got to get away from witch-hunting.'

Mr Frank Williamson, a former member of the Home
Office's Inspectorate of Constabulary, said in an interview
in *The Guardian* on 16 January 1973, after his retirement,
that every respectable policeman would welcome the
existence of a squad

'. . . that guarantees that every policeman who needs dealing
with will be dealt with. And it also has a positive function.
The greatest deterrent is the certainty of detection, and
that applies to policemen as well as anyone else. A detective who gets his sticky fingers on "bent" money is going
to think twice and probably stop if he feels there is a
possibility of being caught in the act and losing the money
as well as his job. That may be cynical, but that's the
way it is'.

Within the Metropolitan Police there are plenty of
detectives anxious to serve honestly and well. Although
wrongdoing is by no means confined to the CID, it was the
CID which gave most cause for anxiety. In the past, complaints about CID officers were investigated by officers
within the department. This was another symptom of the
way the CID had been allowed to become a force within
a force, with its own brand of group loyalties. This does

not mean that there are not, or were not, excellent men in the CID, but it does mean that the structure of the force was dangerously wrong and that some men went bad more easily than should have been possible.

Nominally, the uniformed commanders of the divisions into which the force is divided geographically were responsible for the CID officers in those divisions, but it was responsibility without adequate power. Before the changes made by Sir Robert, the divisional commander would sometimes find CID men, for whom he was responsible on paper, being moved out without him being informed. If the divisional commander tried to keep a close eye on a detective he felt was not up to standard, other senior CID officers might move him to another division, claiming that, although the detective did not arrest many criminals, he was good at surveillance and passing back information. So, on being moved to friendlier pastures, he would continue to be a detective. The fault was not that senior CID officers wished to keep a poor detective. They merely felt that their work was not properly understood and resented outside interference. Poor detectives could sometimes play upon those loyalties.

It is against that sort of background that Sir Robert's actions must be seen. A lot depends upon him in the next few years. He has gone some of the way, since taking over, towards creating the teamwork necessary for the future health of the force and ensuring, by the promotion of good policemen, that the right spirit endures. But further important changes are still awaited. Sir Robert's real test is to come. His appointment is by the Home Secretary, and it is necessary for him to work closely with the Home Office while retaining independent control of the force – a difficult enough task for anyone. He himself might well retort that there is no question about it – he is independent. But he has yet to demonstrate that independence on an issue of real principle.

III
REMEDIES

7 The Police in a Social Role

The limitations of the police – Lord Devlin in error –
a 'no-go' area in Britain – new cures for crime –
on a police raid in Soho – a policewoman is shocked.

What the police can do by themselves to overcome the major external problems they have to face is limited. The causes of crime, public turbulence and traffic ills have, up to now, lain beyond their direct influence. But as we shall see, they are, in fact, becoming increasingly efficient in their approach to detection.

By using their powers of persuasion and publicity they can encourage people to fit safes that are difficult to burgle, locks that are hard to pick, and alarm systems that will alert them to break-in attempts. These are the paraphernalia and hardware of crime prevention, and crime prevention is seen as a major police task. While the police can, by similar means, encourage motorists to take such elementary precautions as removing ignition keys and locking doors, it is up to manufacturers of cars to fit steering that locks automatically.

Likewise with public turbulence. The Special Branch has a pretty good idea of the people who are likely to stir up trouble as a means of subversion. But agitators have appeal only if the message they preach strikes a chord in the hearts and minds of people with a genuine grievance. The means of removing that grievance do not lie within the powers of the police. The means are political.

It is the same with traffic. The police can do their best to ensure that the streets are free of obstructing vehicles and can keep traffic moving. They can also encourage accident prevention, and, by school visits, alert children to the dangers they must avoid. But measures such as the prohibition of lorries in city centres except for those on business there, the building of better roads, or attempts to persuade people to travel by public transport by means of a pricing policy, are beyond them; although the police can provide facts and advice on which decisions can be based.

Policemen, by nature, like to have culprits: people they can identify as causing trouble. Trouble is defined as behaviour that is against the law. This means catching the culprits, fitting their offences to the appropriate law, and prosecuting the offence. The question of whether the police in fact always choose the appropriate law is a major study in itself. Courts have to be convinced that the culprits have committed an offence. The police approach to subversives is somewhat similar, as the Rudi Dutschke case showed. A picture is built up of a man's movements, associates, the organisation to which he belongs, its aims, objects and publications. While this may give a picture of who is dabbling in what, it is essentially superficial, if the real aim is the removal of the true source of wider public discontent.

There are policemen who are aware of the limitations of the police and who ask if the police role is sufficiently broad. This question is easiest to approach if it is first turned on its head by examining what is too narrow a role for the police. Lord Devlin, in his Frank Newsam lecture at the Police College, Bramshill, argued: 'We should try to get back to the idea that the police are a body that exists to deal with real crime, that the duties they are given to do in the enforcement of social regulations are foreign to their nature, and the less they have to do with them the better.'

It is true that policemen would find obnoxious the task of spying on people to see whether they deserve social security benefits, or that they have got planning permission for a garage. The police themselves have also largely withdrawn from another area of potentially abrasive contact with ordinary people – over parking offences – leaving unpopularity to traffic wardens. And there are policemen who would agree with Lord Devlin that they should exist to deal with real crime. They regard the police as first and foremost thief-takers. The logical extension of this would be greater emphasis being given to the CID, the direct entry of recruits to the CID (which would truly then be the elite of the service), and possibly its becoming dominant over the whole of the police service – which would not be without dangers, as we have seen. Such changes would bring about a fundamental change in the way that the public regard the police. Surveys have shown that they see the police as performing a community service in protecting the citizen and helping him in times of trouble. Although people regard the fight against crime as being important, it comes second in their eyes to looking after the public and is a means to that wider end. Thus, when people think of the police, they have in mind the uniformed man on the beat, rather than the detective. So the first objection to the police being simply thief-takers is that that is not what the public want. And as policing in this country is done via the consent of the public, the objection is important.

The second question is that if the police were there to deal with crime, what priority could then be given to the social tasks that the policeman now performs?

In *The Police We Deserve*, Mr John Alderson agrees with Professor Michael Banton's view that 'the policeman must be someone who helps as well as avenges', at least in the British context. Mr Alderson points out that the police still play a large part in such duties as the prevention of cruelty to children, dealing with diseased animals, the prevention of cruelty to animals, the control of the litter problem, and from time to time also with minor and major incidents ranging from floods to aircraft and rail crashes and tragedies on the scale of the Aberfan disaster. The purely legalistic approach to the function of the police would undoubtedly deprive society of one of its major social services. Indeed, the police station is the only place to which people can turn throughout twenty-four hours in time of trouble.

The third point is that dealing with crime is in any case only part of the job the police are doing. In the Metropolitan Police newspaper, *The Job*, in July 1972, the Commissioner stated that only 3 per cent of police time was actively spent in dealing with crime and criminals. (This does not mean that more of it ought not to be spent in this way, but clearly something else would have to suffer, if different priorities were given.)

The fourth point is that Lord Devlin's idea would be against the traditional role of the police and as originally conceived. Enforcement of the law to the exclusion of a lot else would inevitably lead to the police viewing people largely in terms of who was a potential criminal and who was not, seeking remedies only with the law. This would in turn give the police a harsher image. Early Chief Constables were as concerned with that as their successors are now. The Chief Constable of Liverpool told his recruits in 1852, in a classic piece of advice:

'Kite-flying in the streets is a very dangerous practice; and if the string breaks and the kite flaps in the face of a horse, it will frighten it; the horse may injure himself, kill his rider, and seeing how crowded the crossings of our public thoroughfares are, cause great danger to many. The kite is almost always in the hands of a very little boy or girl, bought probably with a penny given by a next door neighbour. To bring such a little creature before the magistrates would never do, although it is an offence against the bye-laws. To put a stop to flying kites, one constable of rough disposition snatches the kite, snaps it in two, at which every person passing will say, "What a horrid fellow that is; the police are not at all a good sort of men." Another constable, seeing the same thing, will call out in a pleasant voice, "My little lad (or lass) go to the fields and fly your kite there, it may cost a man his life flying it in the street"; thus showing the public that, while the constable has his duty to do, he has some regard for what people think of him. The opinion of the public is often formed by the single act of the single individual, whether rough or smooth.'

The police never have existed to deal with crime only to the extent that Lord Devlin believes in. His concept is wrong in fact and would be injurious in principle. Mr Alderson would wish the police to be social diagnosticians, indicating points of strain in society, so that social agencies can be mobilised to help, thus alleviating trouble and distress which might have resulted in police action anyway. Mr Alderson's idea is a development of the best traditions of preventive policing. The police already fulfil this role to some extent, though on a narrower basis as yet. The following example illustrates this approach. A recently widowed lady in her 80s, living by herself in Watford, was unwell, and a local church minister alerted the police. Regularly, two policewomen called on her to see how she was. The minister was a black man and she white, which also showed the way that integration can work at its best.

Admirable though this service was, there was a need for the police to be alerted by a member of the community before they reacted. By themselves they would never have heard about the case, because their own contact with the community was not that close. It was to try and partly overcome the effects of that gap that the home beat scheme was introduced. Policemen are given areas of their own to work, backed up by all the specialist resources that, these days, can be brought to bear. The trouble with some of these home beats is that they are too large. In the Notting Hill area of London, these 'local' policemen have been distributing printed cards, giving their names, inviting the public to contact them in time of need and informing them how to do this.

In some places, such as Cardiff's Tiger Bay, that social role of the police has always been strong, though stern. Tiger Bay's teeth have now been drawn by redevelopment, job mobility and greater prosperity than thirty years' ago. Those days the police are said to have walked in pairs. Tiger Bay can still be pretty tough, but with the decline of Cardiff as a seaport and of the coal trade, its reputation has softened.

Chief Superintendent William Williams, who was stationed there, told the Select Committee on Race Relations and Immigration: 'I have been connected with the police for thirty-eight years.' He added of relations between the police and people there: 'Years ago, they were part police and part social workers. If there was domestic trouble the police were called and the police sorted it out. The coloured people had faith in the police. This is the kind of attitude I at least try to foster now.' Elsewhere, policemen in tough areas have said that mothers still brought along their children to the police station to be chastised.

Today, policemen are unlikely to make chastisement physical. Instead children are in greater danger of being hauled up before the juvenile court, in which case the bureaucracy of the law takes over. The only record of a cuff round the ear was a certain soreness, which soon wore off. Police officers, like the Chief Constable of Liverpool in 1852, are aware of the need to keep young children who have not committed very serious offences out of the records. The juvenile bureau system, in which children are formally admonished by a police officer of some seniority as a warning, so that an eye can be kept on them, is tacit recognition of this. But there is also some feeling among the police that the sanctions open to the court against some juveniles are not sufficient. In Scotland, the social role of the police is more formalised, with a specialist branch handling not only juvenile liaison and community relations, but crime prevention as well. Ayrshire is particularly lively in this respect, seeking not only the active participation of the community, but also involving its leaders in thought-provoking seminars on various ills of society which lead to police involvement.

Much of the stimulus for this emphasis on the social

role comes from Mr David Gray, H.M. Chief Inspector of Constabulary for Scotland. He possesses a capacity for probing at the real causes of events that give rise to police activity, an ability to play his cards well, and a genuine compassion that gives policing a human face. The idea is not that involvement with the community should be left to the specialists but that they should provide the spark and guidance for the rest of the service.

The way this works is well illustrated in Blackhill, one of Glasgow's toughest slums, to which the first bus ran in April 1973. Blackhill had been the nearest thing in Glasgow to a 'no-go' area. The bus drew in next to gaunt buildings in a scene of grim desolation opposite a police office which was opened in April 1972. The bus and the police office were two outward signs that Blackhill seemed to be on the way at last to rehabilitation. The absence of a bus service and hostility, sometimes violent, towards outsiders, illustrated how Blackhill had failed to fulfil its original object of integrating people, cleared from the slums in the 1930s, into the wider community. Instead, Blackhill itself became virtually a segregated slum. But among those gaunt buildings lived decent people too. For years they had tried to maintain standards against dismaying odds. Until the arrival of the police office, there had been no usable telephone kiosks. Vandals had put them and the one police box out of action. At night, picked policemen had stood outside shops to prevent looting. Shopkeepers had secured their premises with steel shutters or had built brick frontages, adding to the impression that this was an area under siege.

Mr Gray said: 'Thanks largely to the imagination and initiative of Glasgow's Chief Constable, Mr David McNee, a police presence has been established, and thus the basis provided for the community to pull itself up by its bootstraps. Policemen would not go in there alone at night.' Anyone going in on business concerned with collecting money and not known in the area ran the risk of being robbed. Out of nearly 4,000 people who lived there about 2,000 had criminal records, he said. The buses had not run because of the likelihood of damage to them.

It was difficult to collect rents and 'moonlighting' of families who had built up arrears was frequent; in less than a year, Mr Gray said, 169 families had left in debt. Those difficulties were being overcome. The police office was opened behind a solid brick frontage. In the entrance is now a telephone kiosk, watched over by the police, where local people can make calls.

Building on the wish of decent people in Blackhill to improve life there, the police, working closely with councillors and corporation officials, secured a football pitch and the creation of a general play area. Youths were organised to remove litter. A street football league was formed, and use of a school pool enabled the formation of a swimming club. All those activities were under the supervision of adult members of the community with voluntary participation by police officers.

Nineteen of the twenty Scottish police forces had by mid-1973 set up community involvement branches, staffed by no more than a fiftieth of the police strength. That means that there were no more than 200 officers in the branch in the whole of Scotland. But Blackhill also implies a recognition that trying to involve the community is of little use if the community itself is underdeveloped. Where this is so, as in Blackhill, the Scottish police, at least, are prepared to help in building up the community itself.

Though police in London have not gone as far in actively building up the community as in Scotland, the problem is recognised. The idea of social diagnosis was introduced experimentally in 'N' Division, where a policewoman was posted to maintain contact with problem families living in an area so as to alert other social agencies to potential trouble points that would need police attention. Again the intention was prevention.

A similar idea was taken a stage further in 'E' Division, where Inspector Jane Folan has been working particularly closely with other social agencies. It was through her initiative that twenty-two of them were got together to discuss a particular block that was causing trouble. The suggested outcome was to use one of the housing units to accommodate a social worker on duty. It was something like the Blackhill project in miniature.

Sometimes it is too late for police to be able to prevent youngsters setting out on the path to trouble and they have instead to be rescued as they are about to fall into it. There is close liaison between police and welfare organisations who meet girls at the big railway stations and try to provide them with help before they fall into wrong hands. Vice-rings have traditionally found railway termini a fruitful source of recruits, as young girls on their first trip alone to London are eager, in the words of the cliché, for the bright lights. These days the attraction seems more to be darkness. Darkness and noise is what so-called night clubs have to offer superficially in the Soho area at night.

One typical operation to pull in young people needing care and protection involved a team of five uniformed women officers, three uniformed policemen, and two plain-clothes men, going into Soho from 1.50 a.m. to 3.15 a.m. Their green bus stopped first near Piccadilly Circus. The officers got out quickly and filed into an amusement arcade, wandering between the people playing machines, scanning faces and trying to pick out likely juveniles. A policewoman went up to a boy, an Asian playing a fruit machine, and stood, hands on hips, asking him questions. Not convinced he was over age (normally 17, but 18 if the subject of a care order), she gripped his arm above the elbow, went with him to the cashier, who was trying his best to look impassive, where the lad cashed the tokens he had, and then she accompanied him back to the bus.

Travelling quickly into the seedier areas of Soho, the squad went into cafés and another amusement arcade, the policewomen asking ages and quickly following up with a request for the date of birth. If there was hesitancy, or the date was not known, they asked further questions. The principle is the same as asking the driver of a car for its number, to explore whether he really is the owner.

One coloured youth, who looked weary, unkempt and unshaven, was asked his age, and then date of birth, but the two did not match up, so he was taken firmly, but politely, through the side door of a club down to the bus. In a café, Sergeant M. Woodheath, who was aged twenty-four and leading the patrol, came across two young men. They said that they were RAF apprentices, so she looked at their identity cards and leave passes, asking them how old they were. They told her they had nowhere to stay. 'The people back at camp wouldn't be happy with you spending your time just hanging around like this, would they?' she said. 'It's not very impressive, is it?' Satisfied with their replies, her official poker face relaxed into a reassuring smile. 'Got enough money?' They nodded.

Emerging from the noisy darkness of a club, Sergeant Woodheath said: 'Did you see that girl in there in the spotted dress? I have known her since she was twelve. The Social Services advised us when she was sixteen-and-a-half not to bring her any more to the station. She was a hopeless case, determined to be a prostitute. Now she's making a bomb.'

Back in the police station, Sergeant Woodheath restored a straying wisp of hair under her uniform hat and faced the youngsters the squad had brought in. They included eight boys, two of them coloured (one Asian) and two coloured girls. She told them that no-one would go until their ages, names, addresses, etc. had been verified, so she advised them to co-operate.

The round-up was gradually discovered to include five adults (over 17) and eleven juveniles. Two, aged 16, were absentees while on Borstal licence and five were juveniles who had come up to London for the night and were collected by their parents who had been informed by the police. In the previous ten months there had been ten sweeps, with a total of 109 youngsters brought in. Thirty-one were aged between 17 and 18 and classed as adults, and 15 were missing persons under the age of 17. Another five missing persons were dealt with eventually by the courts as being in need of care and control. Twenty-three were absentees from care. Twenty-six were ordinary juveniles. Three of the 109 were wanted persons, one for theft and two for breaking and entering offences. Four were arrested for unlawful possession of drugs and two of those were found to be juveniles. Two more were absconders while on Borstal licence.

Sergeant Woodheath said:

'Many are juveniles who missed the last transport home. They get stuck up here and involved with undesirables. We are really looking for the ones who are missing. We get them from as far away as Scotland, Ireland and Wales. In the summer, they can sleep in the parks. They can spend all night in a café, or go from a café to a club and back to a café. Most of the persistent absconders know they would be picked up at the railway stations and so avoid them. If they are young lads, men will start speaking to them, take them back to their homes and be nice to them. They are usually naive, these lads, and often accept. The man demands something more of them. Eventually, they put these lads on the streets as male prostitutes, and they give the men part of their earnings. Their ages can range from 14 upwards. Many of these boys end up as "homos" permanently. When they first arrived in London they were quite normal boys. If they had been for some time with the man who originally picked them up, they may resent him and go to another area and stay with someone else. We collect these young lads on this sort of operation.

'It is very difficult to get at the man behind them. Boys are reluctant to give a description, or name and address. They are frightened to give you much. Occasionally they will, and the CID will investigate that. Everybody in the game knows everybody. One man had ten little boys working as prostitutes for him from 14 upwards. They were reluctant to give evidence. Some didn't turn up at the court. But others did and he was convicted.

'If they have been missing from home a short time and are not involved in anything immoral and their parents want them back, they go home. If the parents don't want them or are not concerned, we put them into children's homes and seek the advice of the social services. Then they decide with the help of the local social services – local, that is, to where the child came from – whether it is best for the child to go home, or into a children's home, or go before a court. All of us try to avoid taking a child before a court, but sometimes this has to happen. This is because we all think the child is in need of care and control. We have a period of eight days from the time they are found to decide what to do with them.'

Sergeant Woodheath had been in the police for four-and-a-half years and remained very feminine although, as her contact with Soho showed, she was capable of exercising natural authority. She knew when to turn the pertinent, straight-faced question into a reassuring, helpful smile. She said about her job:

'I was shocked at first. I came more or less straight from school. I had worked at Scotland Yard. I was very green. I missed a lot at first (referring to duty in Soho) because I didn't know what to go for. It is from the young people you learn so much. They don't realise how deeply in it they are. They don't understand it. The most shocking thing is the damage that is done to them for the rest of their lives. Also, when they reject their parents.

'When we have picked up these young people, I have seen girls whose parents have come from Newcastle and Glasgow, say, and the child won't even speak to them or see them. That is very upsetting. You sometimes ask West Indian children, "Who is your father?" And they say, "Which one?" '

The added emphasis on the social role has caused some misunderstanding within the police. Mr James Starritt, Deputy Commissioner of the Metropolitan Police, said of the system in which a policeman was given an area in which he could be a local 'bobby': 'The first problem was that some of them began to think that they were not policemen, but community workers. If you get a chap who knows everyone and they bring him their problems, you may think to yourself that he has become more of a community worker than policeman. He has to be both. . . . I feel that this has been very successful in various areas.'

Occasionally, the two roles of the police – thief-taker and local 'bobby' – come into conflict. Mr Starritt gave an example:

'At Kentish Town there was a group of hippie communes. The local home beat officer had good relations with the members of these communes and this contact was of value in such everyday matters as tracing missing teenage girls and acquiring other information. There was, however, a bad crime situation in the general locality which resulted in the Special Patrol Group being called in to bring about an improvement. In the course of their ordinary patrol, the Special Patrol Group arrested several hippie commune members for drug offences. After that, there was a breakdown in confidence and the home beat officer was denied access to the communes. A balance has to be kept, but all in all talking to people is very important. As a distinguished barrister is once alleged to have said to a judge: "You may not be any wiser, but you are better informed." '

The same sort of dilemma occurs over whether or not to prosecute in cases of baby-bashing. Another senior policeman replied that he would first ask the community liaison officer to try and find out as much as he could about the case. 'We have discretion,' the senior officer said. 'I would rather get to hear about it at this stage when something constructive can be done than at an inquest of the child.' The community liaison officer added:

'The argument against police involvement is that the police will come along and arrest the parents who are just as much a social and medical case as the child. The argument is: What is the good of arresting the father and putting him away for six months where he can't provide for the family and his support is removed? But that, in our view, is not a reason for calling in the police too late.'

Some social workers do not like the police to be involved in a social role, saying they do not have the specialised training. Police refute this, some replying that social workers want to mould people body and soul rather than letting them develop gradually on their own terms. The fact is that the best policemen care deeply about people under stress with whom they come into contact. Good officers are also shrewd and can apply common sense, which they often think better, after some years of experience, than the theories applied by a social worker straight from her studies. One old provincial policeman called them 'mini-skirted wonders'.

The most difficult task of the community liaison officer is how to bridge the gap between the thinking of some black people, especially the young, and the police. Just as the police generally are sometimes in a buffer role between the government and the protesting, so the community liaison officer may find himself, if he is not careful, in a purely buffer role between the police and aggrieved black people. In this position, he tends to become isolated within the police force. 'Practical coppers' may think that the business of getting on with the less friendly black people can be left to him. 'That's what he's paid for, isn't it?' one such policeman said.

To ask a community liaison officer to get over this isolation by himself sets him an impossible task. He has to be backed firmly by his superiors and efforts made to penetrate that corporate feeling, within the police, that, as we have seen, contributes to their sense of identity. They remain 'tribalistic'. And this can present difficulties. The reason is explained by Chief Inspector Jennifer Hilton in *The Police We Deserve,* as we noted earlier, and her views are worth expanding.

'The tendency in a society with no apparent consensus of opinion is for separate groups, such as the police, to establish their own norms of behaviour.

'There is ample experimental evidence to show how strong the influence of such group norms can be, and how difficult it is for individuals to stand against them. Few people are willing in a closed community, such as the police service, to express opinions or beliefs that are at variance with those of their colleagues. Not only group norms of behaviour are established, but also stereotyped opinions about race and class. To break the unwritten taboos is not only to incur the displeasure of one's fellows, but is also to feel distress and tension within oneself. . . . Police behavioural norms that are generally admired are those of rapid, decisive action and "tough" rather than "soft" behaviour. The man who makes arrests (even unnecessarily) is thought more admirable than the man of honeyed tongue who resolves all his disputes into "no cause for police action".'

This may explain the reason not only for the conflict, to which Mr Starritt refers, between the thief-taking and social roles of the police, but it also indicates what an uphill task some of the community liaison officers have. Chief Inspector Hilton adds penetratingly:

'Psychology has had much to say about those groups in society which do not conform to the usual norms and these are often the groups with whom police officers have most dealings.

'A police officer may feel less constrained by normal

patterns of behaviour, if the people he is dealing with are vagrants or some other outcast groups such as hippies or drug-addicts that society (as he knows it) treats with little respect. There are dangers in the labelling and identifying of such sub-groups in society. Criminals, alcoholics, vagrants, madmen and delinquents – the mad, the bad and the sad – each group has its own particular image or stereotype that tars all its individual members with the same brush.'

In other words, they are all 'slag', in the jargon we earlier discussed – the jargon of the police sub-group. And, as we have seen, it is by stereotyping that the police know how to spot, for instance, thieves on wheels. The police label not only the 'slag' but also the respectable. If the police are also a 'sub-group', they too will be labelled, identified and stereotyped. This means that they, too, will become a target of hostility for some people. In those circumstances, it becomes the more difficult for the police to fulfil the social role which has long been theirs.

Thus the nature of the police, which we explored in Section II, has direct bearing upon their ability to do the sort of tasks they are called upon to perform.

8 The Thief-takers

Strategic planning against crime – how a major crime operations room works – tackling the racket in antiques – why people become informers – the tedious reality of murder investigation – the weakness of international policing.

The strategy of the police in detecting crime is like that of any other business: to identify the main targets and bring organised, skilled and determined resources to bear against them. The most successful criminals do the same in planning their operations. A main target of the police strategy is the professional criminal, either in a gang or organised in a group, and the violent offender. The story of how the police smashed the Krays' and Richardsons' gangs is well known. They ruled by fear, and the problem was to get witnesses to come forward, so that sufficient evidence could be levelled against the villains. In cases of this sort and those involving the new breed of more sophisticated criminals, the modern police approach is to use groups of officers to keep surveillance on individuals, so that scraps of information can be pieced together to form evidence of their associates and actions.

It was for this reason that regional crime squads were formed. There are nine in the country, which they cover geographically. The modern key to both the strategy and tactics of detection is the obtaining and classifying of criminal intelligence. To gain it, the police need informants. Sometimes the police will themselves place undercover men in organisations. The Flying Squad at Scotland Yard has long worked, like the regional crime squads, on the principle of observing professional criminals.

Specialist crimes require specialist squads. The Bomb Squad, the Fraud Squad, the Art and Antiques Squad and the Drug Squad are examples. One of the newest of the specialist groups of detectives is the Robbery Squad. It came into being to deal with a vast increase in bank robberies. In 1971, the number of bank robberies in which a bank itself was the loser doubled to forty without any corresponding increase in arrests. And there were more bank robberies in the first half of 1972 (forty-two) than in the whole of the previous year. The Commissioner, Sir Robert Mark, called a top-level conference and gave a briefing on broad strategy. This was, for the first time, to use the combined resources of the Regional Crime Squad, the Divisional CID and Criminal Intelligence in one specialised squad, supported directly by the uniformed and traffic branches.

Although groups for special tasks are obviously desirable as a means of building up expertise and knowledge, each group had in the past tended to cling on to its own jealously. Not only was the CID in the Metropolitan Police a 'force within a force', but within the CID there were lots of little 'firms' – a word used by police themselves with innocent connotations as applied here, though borrowed from slang for small criminal empires.

The Flying Squad had felt uncertain of its future when Sir Robert Mark took over as Commissioner. Symptomatic of its frustration was a notice on the wall of its office saying: 'We trained hard ... but it seemed that every time we were beginning to form up into teams we would be reorganised. I was to learn later in life that we tend to meet any new situation by reorganising; and a wonderful method it can be for creating the illusion of progress while producing confusion, inefficiency and demoralisation – Petronius Arbiter 210 B.C.' Perhaps the Flying Squad should have been more careful in choosing their particular 'informant'.

There was no reference to Petronius Arbiter in the Oxford Classical Dictionary that fitted the time of 210 B.C. But there was one around at the time of Nero, Roman Emperor from A.D. 54–68. Petronius Arbiter, says the dictionary, became a master of the Emperor's pleasures – 'a delicate voluptary, lending a certain elegance to the corrupt court, whose distractions lacked refinement'. He was alleged to have been in a conspiracy against Nero and came to a sticky end. He wrote a document denouncing the Imperial vices with the names of his accomplices, and then, in the words of the dictionary, enjoyed an elegant suicide. Not the sort of authority the Flying Squad should cite.

The success of the Robbery Squad and the importance being placed upon the role of the Flying Squad have done much to raise morale again. The way they (and other special squads) work well illustrates the degree of organisation needed to solve big crimes these days. The senior detective has to be as much manager as sleuth. Let us have a look at the operations' room in action against the perpetrations of a major crime. Thirty-two policemen were involved in the day-to-day operations, though this represented only part of the effort. Many hundreds of telephone calls were received following a television appeal for information on 'Police 5', the programme which seeks help from the public for information about crimes.

Each call was carefully and briefly noted on separate sheets of paper and given an action number, so that it was possible to see precisely at any one moment what had resulted. The messages and action taken were logged in a book. A blackboard at one end of the room had on it a list of detectives involved in the case. Against their names were the action numbers they were allocated to deal with.

A pink blob against a detective's name meant that he was a trained marksman. The philosophy of the Force on weapon training is that it is better to teach a man how to use a gun properly than to have an untrained man killing people because he cannot aim straight. The twenty-three marksmen involved were no more and no less than a reflection of the violence in society today and the possibility of its use in the crimes being investigated. But it had not been necessary to issue a gun to any of the police in the squad up to the time of the visit for the purposes of this description. The decision to do so would be taken by the senior officer involved.

The results of the action taken by the detectives on item numbers against their names were recorded, even if it resulted in nothing. Minute, and what might have seemed at the time to be unimportant, information was transferred to a crime index. This was a card filing system. The cards were headed with the kind of information received – telephone numbers, or car types, or other appropriate tags. If different people replying to the 'Police 5' request or other publicity had seen and noted a car in different places with a particular number, a card was opened on it, so that information about it could be built up. It may have been that the only details remembered by a witness were its type and colour. A card would be opened nevertheless, so that, as more information came in, it would be possible to be more specific. Telephone numbers were pieced together similarly from scraps of information. Sometimes informants in clubs may remember a particular call being made. If, say, a red duffle bag was mentioned in an interview, it would be underlined in red in the action book and a card would be made out for it in the index, referring to the action number. So, if other people mentioned a red duffle bag later, information about it would be added to the file.

Several copies of statements taken, perhaps as a result of a call, were made, so that they could be filed into books, with a reference number for each person. Each day the officer in charge read new statements.

Within seconds of, say, a red duffle bag becoming important in a case, it would be possible to turn up all reference to it from the filing system. Officers, by going back through the files of previous cases, might pick up a reference to it there. Exhibits may not only be of value to one case under investigation in, say, a series of unsolved murders, but may, by being linked to other people and events, be the clue needed to crack a previously unsolved case. In a room next to the operations room were the exhibits where, eventually, the red duffle bag might turn up. If it did, it would be examined thoroughly and perhaps sent to the forensic laboratories.

This illustrates the way in which information is pieced together in dealing with major crime. Although much depends upon the officer in charge, nothing could be achieved without a system of organisation. Solving crime depends also upon narrowing down the area of search, so that you know precisely where to look. This is the method used in the Art and Antiques Squad, which was formed in 1968. Then, an average of £90,000 stolen items a month were being lost. The figure at the end of 1972 was down to a little over £30,000. The problem seemed to be containable, which made it different from most others facing the police. The reason was that the world of antiques is relatively small, and it is a world in which expensive items are recognisable, unlike, say, whisky stolen from a lorry.

The squad was run in early 1973 with extraordinary panache by Detective Sergeant Sidney Wisker (since retired). Like the other squads at the Yard, the Art and Antiques had taken on something of the character of the world in which it moved. Mr Wisker, talking with enthusiasm about a rare piece of porcelain, looked precisely the sort of man who would pop out from behind a Victorian dresser to sell you a silver spoon or two. (Similarly, Deputy Assistant Commissioner Crane, in charge of the Fraud Squad, had the quiet suit, quiet voice, quiet manner and quiet gaze suited to the hushed interior of a city bank.)

Mr Wisker used publicity in seven trade journals to portray and describe stolen goods. He referred to a photograph of a Hepplewhite chair in one magazine and said that the publicity given to it was responsible for clearing up fourteen jobs and the recovery of £40,000 worth of property and the arrest of two people. 'From these periodicals', he said, 'we get back £70,000 worth of property a year. We have got back £93,000 this year – a good one. A bloke phoned me from Bristol this morning at 9.30 a.m.

He said he had bought an incense burner he thought
might have been stolen in 1971.' Mr Wisker said that the
secret, apart from the publicity, was:

'. . . you have to sell yourself to the trade. It is very conservative. You have to convince them it is for their benefit.

'People say, "Don't you find the antique trade crooked?"
They don't need to be crooked. They can earn so much
money by going straight. With a good furniture dealer,
you could stand a piece of furniture 100 yards away and
he would tell you whether it was right or wrong. He
would say, "Well – they hadn't started on that forest when
that piece was supposed to have been brought out." They
can tell a lot from the wood. If it's a wet climate, it causes
the pores to open out. If it's dry, the wood is tight and
gnarled. These type of people want a clean trade. You
must never cause that man in the middle to mistrust you.
Once you do, you have lost the rest of them. . . .

'If you look at antiques as a pyramid, at the bottom are
market traders, crooks and all the bits and pieces. Say
you put a nice clock in at the bottom. The dealer knows
someone a quarter of the way up the pyramid who knows
a good class clock. He may equally know that to get good
class money he will go straight to the top. So in three
moves the clock will go to the top of the pyramid. There
are 40,000 dealers at the bottom of the pyramid, 20,000
half-way up, and at the top of the pyramid there's one.
It's that sort of man who's anxious that the trade shall be
clean.

'The chap at the top will phone us and say: "Have you
got a Quare missing?" "Yes, we have a bracket clock missing. Is it a verge movement?" "Yes," he says. The chances
are that if it is that good, you have a photograph of it anyway. You say, "Who did you buy it from?" "I bought it
from a clock dealer down the Lane." Then you go to him
and say, "Where did you get it from?" "A chap who goes
round the markets. He says he bought it from a stall in
the so-and-so market." So you go there and the chap there

says: "Guv'nor, I haven't got a bloody clue where I bought it." You say, "Guv'nor, get your coat on. You're nicked." '

Mr Wisker added: 'We have recovered £12 million in four years. A Knib, long-case clock was nicked from the V & A. So I phoned two or three people in the clock trade. They had all got phone calls from people about this Knib who are trying to flog it. It was too hot to handle. So they put it in a box, packed it up nicely, and put it on the steps of the Chelsea nick. Another lot left a collection of pistols at Euston Station.'

When asked if he would nick one of his contacts if he had done something wrong, Mr Wisker replied: 'Yes, you can't have the informant tail wag the police dog.' The use of informants was further explained by Commander J. Lock, head of the Flying Squad, which depended on getting information from people who would speak to a detective only if they knew him and understood him, he said. 'It is rare for an officer to pass on his informants. If the detectives are working together, information is built up in the team as a whole.' There was a sense of 'understanding' between the informer and the policeman, he added. Some obviously gave information because of vindictiveness towards others in the underworld. Others, because they might think they could get some money out of it.

'We have got some very strict instructions about informers participating in crime,' Mr Lock said. These were that informants would not do so except in a very, very minor role, and only then if it was necessary so that the whole group could be arrested as the result of his participating. Obviously, he could not be an *agent provocateur*. Sometimes the line was very narrow. It was necessary for the officers concerned to speak to their senior officers, who would say whether the informant should or should not participate. If the man did participate, this would be brought to the notice of the Director of Public Prosecutions or Solicitors' Department, whoever was dealing with the case. Informants' names were not written down, only telephone numbers and perhaps initials. But each officer must make his Detective Inspector aware of who his informants were.

In fact, there are basically four types of police informer. There are those who want to go straight and by being in touch with the police want them to know they are not mixed up in anything shady; this also acts as a form of self-discipline for the informer. There are those who owe the police 'favours', because officers may have spoken up on their behalf in court and saved them from a longer sentence: one Northern detective always makes a point of visiting some of the lesser villains in the cells after they have been sentenced through his evidence. He said: 'I may want their help in future.' Other informers do it for money and a few (and their information has to be carefully evaluated) for revenge.

Sometimes the police may go further than they should in bringing pressure to bear on people to inform, but in officers' opinions for the best of motives – the clearing up of crime. There is a hazy borderline between what is legitimate and illegitimate. In one case, police were alleged to have told a recently released prisoner that they would forget a complaint laid against him if he would provide information that would get any local criminal locked up. There are two ways of looking at this: one is that it is a form of blackmail. The other is that the police are merely exercising their discretion for the greater good. They are merely developing the principle used when a man turns 'Queen's evidence', so that leniency is shown in return for helping to enforce the law: repentance brings the possibility of forgiveness. This is, however, a false argument. Justice should not constitute people fearing threats.

Watching suspects, as the men of the Flying Squad do, can be tedious and boring. The detective may have to work fifteen hours a day following a suspect in a car, or waiting for a bank raid and seeing, perhaps, a dummy run on it. It is a split-second decision to know whether or not to arrest. If it is a dummy run, then to go in prematurely would mean that an offence had not been committed. On the other hand, not to go in might mean that, if it was an actual bank raid, people's lives might be put at risk.

Just as the Flying Squad gathers information about suspects, so does the commercial intelligence unit of the Fraud Squad keep an eye on suspect companies. And just as fraudsmen form themselves into loose syndicates for particular operations, so the policemen investigating them form units which draw in experts. An example is long term fraud, the system in which credit is built up and then the people in charge of the firm run away with the newly delivered goods. The police have their specialists in the subject. There are other units to deal with frauds associated with inertia selling and pyramid selling, and an international unit.

In addition to the ninety-five officers in the Metropolitan Police on fraud squad duties, there were thirty at the end of 1972 in the City of London under the same joint operational umbrella. Though the City of London force is completely independent, its officers may investigate in some cases in the Metropolitan area and Metropolitan officers do likewise in the city. Scotland Yard's experts can be called in by any Chief Constable, but there are now thirty-nine fraud squads in the country, some of them consisting of only two men.

What puzzles outsiders is how a detective without specialist qualifications in accountancy can detect complicated frauds which, to be successful, have, of course, to conceal the truth. It is said that the ideal fraud detective should be a combination of a lawyer, an accountant and detective. None of the Fraud Squad officers are qualified accountants, though there is an argument for saying that they should be. The Royal Canadian Mounted Police sends its officers away for training on a formal contract to come back for a period afterwards (otherwise it might lose them). In Britain there are, however, courses in fraud investigation and finance which detectives can attend.

In practice, the basic principle in the detection of fraud is rather like that used by a policeman on the beat to prevent crime – he is looking for something that stands out as unusual in a pattern of events or behaviour. Sherlock Holmes, in one of the Conan Doyle stories, found a clue in the dog that did not bark in the night.* Detectives acquire expertise by experience and tuition within the field by getting to know the broad principles of accountancy. Then by living with a set of books and asking questions, they find out how they work, learning the company's system. From then on it is sheer hard work. The Fraud Squad is recognised as a good place in which to train a young detective because he has to have patience and the ability to sort out important items from a mass of detailed information.

Some of the specialist expertise is provided by the Department of Trade and Industry in cases in which it has an interest, when it appoints its own investigator or an outside investigator, or QC. In bankruptcy cases liquidators also provide expertise. Fraud Squads can call on the services of an accountant, though this has been done on only one occasion by the Joint Fraud Squad in recent years. Where the Department of Trade is investigating by virtue of its powers under the Companies' Act, liaison with the Fraud Squad is so close that it amounts almost to a joint investigation.

An accountant may not always have the expertise, in the view of case-hardened detectives, to be able to withstand the attack of counsel in court. Forensic scientists, who are used to court appearances, are used in fraud, as they might be in murder. Both murder and fraud inquiries require immense pains to be taken. This need contributes towards

---

* 'Is there any point', the Inspector asked, 'to which you would wish to draw my attention?' 'To the curious incident of the dog in the night-time.' 'The dog did nothing in the night-time.' 'That', Sherlock Holmes replied, 'was the curious incident.'

a misleading impression given by some top detectives, who appear to display slow and dogged perseverance rather than brilliance. For authors, this makes an ideal contrast with the scintillating hero of detective fiction. But the sort of clues which in reality piece together a solution need extreme care, firstly to discover them and then to preserve them. This comprehensive care is the more necessary now that science has so much to offer in police work. The result is that murder investigation is almost mundane in its attention to detail, rather than glamorous, to the people actually participating. As Frederick Oughton says in *Murder Investigation*, '. . . the murder whose investigation did not require the laboratory examination of evidence has not yet been committed'.

Mr Oughton described how, in one case, an innocent man could have been convicted because of the carelessness with which an officer dispatched evidence to the laboratory for examination. Traces of semen were found on the underclothes of the victim of murder and rape. He wrapped them up with the underpants and trousers of the suspect and sent them off to the laboratory. The laboratory confirmed that dried semen was indeed on the woman's underclothes and 'powdered traces' on the man's. Under examination by defending counsel in court, the laboratory technician concerned said it was quite feasible for the dried semen to have cracked and for powdered traces to permeate the man's garments. Generally, as is shown also by the way other specialist squads work, the successful conclusion of a case depends much upon teamwork, although flair, astuteness and keen observation are, of course, vital within it.

An example of the painstaking inquiries demanded of the police was the clue which led to a man being sentenced to life imprisonment in Reading on 25 July 1973. Mr Justice Thesiger afterwards commended Detective Superintendent Philip Fairweather for efforts to check the murder weapon, a key exhibit in the prosecution case. Detectives traced the gun's history back to 1944, when a soldier picked it up in a trench in France where it had been left behind by a retreating German. The pistol passed through the ownership of eight people before it ended up in the hands of the accused man. He was said to have put two bullets into a man who owed him money on used car deals. The accused denied the murder. It was known that he had bought the pistol from a friend. During their inquiries police found a man who had used the same pistol in competition shooting at Bisley and had kept the cartridges. These matched the ones found at the scene of the crime.

The benefits of specialisation are obvious. The weaknesses are that, in a situation of manpower shortage, the creation of specialist squads contributes to it by siphoning off men from more general duties. Yet, in some cases, the specialist squads may have been created to overcome the effect of the shortage. An example is the Special Patrol Group of the Metropolitan Police. Mr James Starritt said that it was originally formed to help divisions of the Force with particular problems because they did not have enough of their own men. The Special Patrol Group is self-supporting with its own wireless network and personnel carriers. The aim is to provide manpower quickly or to flood an area to prevent or deal with crime.

The Group has been criticised for its heavy-handedness. Colin McGlashan described it in the *New Statesman* of 13 October 1972 as 'the Met's paratroopers'. In fact, he added, its organisation and operational style more clearly resembled, and, indeed, appeared to be based on, American police units like Chicago's Task Force.

But Mr Starritt said:

'They are not the heavy mob, the Hermann Goering Corps, and they will not be. We are very conscious of this and we do not say that the Special Patrol Group must always be on duty when demonstrations are on. But if it gets out of hand, we can call them in, provided they are on duty. They are also good at setting up road blocks and this sort of thing.'

Other tasks have included the dragging of ponds, searching for children, and policing scenes of disaster.

Is it a blunt instrument in sensitive areas? 'To date, this is not a problem. . . . We have used them on demonstrations. We recognise the dangers of them being used as a blunt instrument. They are not on it permanently, although there is no fixed period for service in the Group. Nor have they been given visor shields and strengthened helmets, but are dressed the same as other officers.' No unit of the Group is in fact autonomous, as each answers to the Chief Superintendent in command, and he in turn must answer to his own Commander and Divisional Commanders. The Group operates on divisions at the request of Commanders and under their directions.

The Group was indeed carefully briefed when it went into one area with sensitive race relations. There was a crime problem in the division and the divisional Commander felt that not to be able to use the Group for the task for which it was intended would be a tacit admission that his division had become a 'no-go' area for them. His argument to the black community and those involved in race relations was that, to give them policing different from other areas would be to discriminate racially against them.

The present awareness of the drawbacks of using the Group in sensitive situations contrasts with the row that developed in Kentish Town, where officers from the Group clashed with members of a commune in June 1972. A street concert ended in fierce struggles and fifteen men appeared in court charged with obstruction and assault on the police. The Group had moved in to the division to crack down on car thefts and burglaries. Mr Ian Litterick, the organiser of Student Community Housing, which had about 100 students in short-life premises owned by Camden Council, alleged harassment by it. He claimed the

Group was victimising anyone with long hair. This the Group would deny.

The real weakness of the Special Patrol Group springs from its functional role used in cracking tough jobs. It is judged by results. But, unlike most other specialist groups of the police, its officers come into contact with the general public on the streets. They see the public mainly in terms of the problem they have come to solve and as potential contributors to that problem. Their view of the public tends, in spite of their general police training and experience, to be one-dimensional, whereas that of the ordinary policeman on patrol in the area is multi-dimensional. He knows the area better, and can more easily make allowances which contribute towards the exercise of discretion – one of the most valuable responsibilities he has. The danger is that a one-dimensional view of the public could enhance some of the latent characteristics already present in the police. As Chief Inspector Hilton indicated in *The Police We Deserve*, those that tend to be admired are those of rapid, decisive action and 'tough' rather than 'soft' behaviour. The Group is known for its 'rapid, decisive action', and whether this is possible without having a feeling of 'toughness' is what raises doubts.

Part of the problem is that no group of officers from a central organisation can have the same sensitive awareness of the local situation as the local policeman. The point is again illustrated by an intensive search for illegal immigrants which caused complaints, again in Camden. As a result, the Home Office admitted that it took place without the knowledge of the local police Commander. Mr Robert Carr, Home Secretary, wrote in reply to a local delegation expressing concern about the effects on relations between police and immigrants:

'Both the Commissioner and I are agreed upon the need for close liaison with the local police in any operation which might have repercussions on relations between the police and the immigrant communities in the area. The

Commissioner will ensure that this takes place in future and that the need to explain the position to members of the local community and the press as soon as this is practicable.'

In this case the raid was conducted by members of the special squad in Scotland Yard dealing with illegal immigrants.

Generally, the experience of all the various specialist groups is that international crime is growing, and improved measures have to be taken to combat it. They use Interpol, which is really a communications system. In addition, they have their own links with their opposite numbers abroad. Detective Sergeant Wisker said: 'I can pick up the telephone and talk to police I know as far away as Japan and New York.'

International crime between Britain and the Continent has become even more tempting since Britain joined the EEC. To curb the international traffic in vehicles, Scotland Yard's special squad dealing with stolen vehicles formed a special group to make swoops on ports. Officers descend on them without warning, to surprise criminals trying to ship stolen vehicles out of Britain. Like any other specialist group at the Yard, it is called in for the more intractable cases requiring its knowledge. Officers in the branch regularly scrutinise the sales columns of newspapers and magazines, to spot sales of vehicles likely to have been stolen. Acting on a hunch, one officer got his wife to answer an advertisement by telephone, went along himself, pretending to be a would-be buyer, inspected the car and telephoned details that were checked against records. As a result, a team of international car thieves was smashed. In another case, the squad swooped successfully on five lorries about to be exported. Two thieves were arrested and convicted.

Law enforcement is becoming increasingly an international exercise, although it is complicated by inadequate laws of extradition, which leave so many loop-holes in the law that the really informed and intelligent criminal could commit some crimes without ever having to pay the price for them. The Home Office is aware that Britain has, on the whole, stood aloof from the Continent in the criminal law field, and extradition is being reconsidered now that Britain is in the Common Market. Negotiating new treaties takes time, although Britain has done so with Denmark and has made arrangements with America to cover the whole gamut of drug offences instead of merely trafficking, as had been the case.

As one policeman said, if the English channel will in the future be no more of a barrier than the Thames has been, it would surely be right to ensure that no criminal who commits an offence in Europe and is caught in Britain has the slightest chance of avoiding justice – any more than would someone caught in Brixton for an Islington house-breaking.

Nor is there any international law to cover fraud. In our laws, it is an offence to conspire to commit an offence abroad, provided the act is provable in this country and the act committed deals with a crime that would be prosecutable in this country. Deputy Assistant Commissioner Crane says:

'Except for a few offences you cannot prosecute United Kingdom citizens in Britain for crimes committed abroad. . . . Fraud, and other such types of crime, are not one of this category of offences. Germany can prosecute in Germany a man who commits a crime abroad, the Scandinavian countries can prosecute similarly the nationals of those countries. In fact, we want to look towards improving our legislation to cater for the fraudster who commits in Britain one link of a chain of events resulting in fraud being committed somewhere else. We have to rely on the good-will of people to come to Britain and give evidence. If they have lost money, they have a strong motive. There are cases where they refuse to come and you cannot make them. The international criminal knows this and is fully aware of the difficulties of prosecution. You would have to have an international police force and an international fraud squad. You have to have international agreement. This is very much a thing for the distant future. Within the Common Market, there is harmonisation of law. There must be an easing of extradition procedures.'

Thus, once more, in a crucial area of operations, the police are subject to external factors beyond their control that can make or mar their success. This is affecting them in their task of thief-taking as it is in controlling traffic or public turbulence.

9   The Computerised Copper

The weakness of the Panda car system – computers
aid policemen – speeding the checks on criminals –
using beetles, flies and foxes as the policeman's friends –
clues in blood, metal and glass – science helps
to solve a crime.

The dilemma of the police about their role is increased
by the complications of present-day society. In the face of
so much and such rapid change, it is understandable that
they should react defensively by clinging on to traditions
and attitudes that have served them well over the years,
to provide them with a platform of stability. They unconsciously withdraw from sensitive areas where abrasive
contact with the public brings them into disrepute and
some would prefer to concentrate on a task which is un-
equivocal – the catching of villains. Here their organisation and intentions are clearest. But because the public
expects them to cater for its well-being in a broader sense,
the police find themselves drawn willy-nilly into some of
the conflicts troubling communities, and here they act
in a buffer role. Because the police do not like to admit
their limitations, they are blamed – and sometimes blame
themselves – for developments and events that are beyond
their power and capability. This lack of definition as to
what their precise role should be is also inhibiting them
from participation in areas, such as environmental planning, where their knowledge and experience would be
valuable. Moreover, in a society in which values have
changed, they feel confused. The surprising thing is that,
despite all the pressures upon them, their attitudes remain
so stable. This may be because, as one senior policeman

put it to me, they retreat into their bastion of Victorianism. There *is* something to be said for it. At their best these qualities have a high-minded worthiness about them, and life, as seen in those black and white terms of right and wrong, is comfortingly simple. The strength of these traditions helps to provide the police with a sense of cohesion and common purpose, though at times this puts them at odds with people of alien life-style.

Those changes are external. Another change is now facing them internally which, unless it is seized with imagination, will add to their defensiveness and sense of dilemma. This change is being wrought by a technological revolution. Like coal-miners, dockers and railwaymen, the police are in a Victorian-based, man-power intensive industry. People in each of those occupations have had to face a similar change, which has transformed them from craftsmen to technicians. Steel is no longer made by hand, as it once was in the hand-mills of South Wales, but is made on computer-controlled production lines. Similarly with coal: the latest developments are towards mechanisation at the pit-face and away from the muscular task of winning coal by picks and shovels. The driver of a modern high-speed train pulls switches and control handles. No-one stokes boilers. The dockers are having to adapt to containerisation. On the railways, in the docks and down the mines there has been strife over pay as the workers react defensively to change and worry about their status.

Most policemen would see themselves primarily as craftsmen. They like to think of themselves as having a personal responsibility for their job and as being able to exercise a distinctive flair in doing it. They would prefer their contact with the public to be of the same kind as that of the village shop-keeper rather than of the manager of a super-market, in which such close personal understanding is less apparent. This is not to say, of course, that the police do not know the value of forensic science, even if, sometimes, they are apt to play it down in conversation. They have been using it for many years. But there is at heart a wish to preserve the human element in policing, and this makes some of them, at least, rather look down upon some of the more wondrous applications of science. This attitude was caricatured by the remark of a senior police officer to his men, when he wished to be known as an old-fashioned practical copper and one of them: 'I don't believe in these new-fangled devices like finger-prints.'

Part of the dilemma facing the police is the wish and need to remain a manpower intensive industry while they are short of men, while life is becoming more complex and criminals more ingenious. That dilemma is exemplified by the saga of the Panda car. Panda cars, which are light blue in colour with a broad white stripe about them, are familiar to everyone. Instead of having a lot of policemen pounding, on foot, beats small enough for each to cover on his own, the Panda enables beats to be increased in size and aid to be summoned swiftly by radio. Pandas enable policemen to get quickly to scenes of trouble and to cover bigger areas.

There have, however, been unfortunate side-effects. The first is that a policeman in a Panda car is removed, during the period he is in it, from contact with people. In theory, policemen should park their Pandas and get out and about a lot. But human nature being what it is, some, to the annoyance of Chief Constables, tend to remain in the comfort of the car, instead of leaving it and exposing themselves to the blast of the elements on wet and windy corners. Nor can a policeman much be blamed if, instead of plodding through the slush in mid-winter, he prefers to keep observation from his car with the heater on. Another drawback is that, at times in recent years, there have not been enough policemen in certain areas to enable the Panda scheme to work properly. Senior officers in some areas have preferred the few available policemen to man the cars as first priority. But one senior policeman said: 'I have always given instructions that men should get out on foot as a priority.' So there have been occasions when valuable investment, in the shape of Panda cars, has been idle in garages.

The second unfortunate effect is that, when manpower is short and beats are big, it is impossible for a policeman on foot always to be near to an incident. The result is a tendency for the police to react in a fire-brigade role, taking pride in reducing the response time. This role is made possible by the improvement in communications. Radios can quickly direct help to the scene of trouble. A lot of policemen do not prefer this role. Their treasured folk memory is still of P.C. Plod rounding their corner and, espying a fracas, proceeding in its direction. Proceeding is a most suitable word, meaning not a walk (which looks unofficial) nor a run (which is undignified) but a steady and resolute approach, giving time for the participants in the trouble to note the majesty of the law on its course and resume a state of orderliness – but not so much time that they have a chance to escape. "Ello, 'ello, 'ello,' rumbles P.C. Plod in tones of fatherly disapproval. 'What's all this 'ere, then?' This gives him an opportunity to be convinced by someone that the half-conscious victim has got a bloody nose, not from a punch, but that he has walked into a door-post by mistake. (A good officer must never believe his own eyes until he has verified his opinions with supporting evidence.) All this acts unconsciously as a dampener of emotions, a sobering influence. 'Now Sir,' says P.C. Plod, turning to the large gorilla of a man with cauliflower ears. Taking out his notebook and deliberately licking his pencil, P.C. Plod asks, 'Would you mind giving your version of this incident, please?'

Of course, it does not happen like that. It never has. But caricaturing a situation does emphasise the salient point. The policeman in those days, being on his own, had to act on his own initiative and defuse difficult situations rather than inflame them.

Now contrast this with a current situation in which a policeman, driving his Panda, notes a crowd of black youths outside a club, pushing each other all over the pavement and cheerfully shouting abuse. Heads crane from windows. Elderly widows, clutching handbags, cross over the road to avoid the fuss. The police officer takes a look and gets on to the radio to headquarters and calls for help as there is, he says, a disturbance in which a crowd of black youths is obstructing the pavement and annoying passers-by. He is young, this policeman, and inexperienced. He thinks it best not to go and sort out the problem, if it is one, by himself. One of the reasons is that he has heard from talk in the police canteen about the sort of people these young blacks are – the amount of mugging they do, their anti-police attitude. Within a few minutes cars arrive with blue lights flashing and sirens blaring, a motor-cyclist roars up revving his engine and braking with a jerk, looking, in his helmet, like some automaton out of space fiction. The police go in. The youths object, protesting that they are doing nothing. And anyhow they have their own ideas of what fascist pigs do to black kids and they determine at all costs not to be arrested, because, they think, they'll have their heads put down lavatory pans with the flush pulled. So there is a nasty, fierce incident. Again, of course, the events are dramatised and oversimplified to make the point.

Many policemen think that there is nothing wrong with the Panda car, provided it is used properly. Some police say there is a tendency to be too quick on the draw in calling up aid, when a practical copper ought to be able to sort things out for himself. But not all police like Panda cars. One officer in a class at the Police College, Bramshill, which was pretty evenly divided about the merits of them, referred to Panda cars as 'bloody ice-cream wagons. Let's get rid of them,' he said.

Mr G. W. R. Terry, when Chief Constable of Lincolnshire, did just that. 'In Lincolnshire', he said, 'the Panda car has been done away with. We have tended to reduce the number of cars and put men on the beat. There was a lack of personal contact with the public. Relations with the public are very good. We have had lots of bouquets over our response time, which we maintain. Although the men on the beat are in close touch with the public, they are also able to get help quickly by radio.'

Mr Terry obviously did not get rid of cars *per se*. His objection was to the rigid principle of Panda policing that was producing a gap with the public on whom the police depended to do their job. 'We became disillusioned with the number of Panda cars to men on the beat,' he said. People thought that they would see a policeman only when there was trouble in a sort of fire-brigade role.' Lincolnshire had the good fortune, however, of being pretty well up to strength.

By doing away with the Panda, Lincolnshire has perhaps come to terms with the police car, for cars are still used, though not so dogmatically. The need for the police to come to terms with technology generally is evidenced by the way that new discoveries are gradually being brought into use.

In comparison with, say, the army, the police have been underdeveloped when it comes to science. Whereas the Ministry of Defence has been spending 10 per cent of its annual overall budget on research and development to try and find new technological aids, similar expenditure for police purposes is still only approximately 0·25 per cent. In the three years up to 1973/4 the expenditure of the Police Scientific Development Branch of the Home Office increased by 50 per cent and will have doubled by the end of 1973/4. The intention is not to change the role of the police. The policy remains to regard them as members of society, and have them mingling with it. Although the police are considered to be doing their job in the right way, they are thought not to be doing it as efficiently as would be possible with modern aids. The job of the Police Scientific Development Branch at the Home Office is to create that efficiency.

The first and most important need is considered to be improvement in management techniques with the aid of modern technology. It is for this purpose that a new method of control, with the help of a computer, has been introduced at Birmingham and is in the process of being installed, too, at Glasgow. Individual forces had been ignoring this sort of new technology, which was understandable because, unlike business and industry, there is no simple means, such as profit, for measuring cost-effectiveness. The way that individual forces are funded – half the money comes from local authorities – inhibits large capital expenditure. The police have not seriously considered leaps into the technological unknown.

It was decided that the best approach was to start with a simple pilot scheme. Methods of command and control were examined world-wide and the United States approach was considered technically right, but its police application wrong. It was also believed to be too revolutionary for police in the U.K. to accept or police financiers to contemplate. The Los Angeles system, for example, cost $58 million.

An evolutionary approach was decided on, using a single computer and the existing system as a fallback. An advantage of this approach is that the police can see exactly what extra facilities they are getting for their extra expenditure. Home Office experts see two areas in which the computer can help. The first is to hold information about all the resources available for deployment and to display it in such a way that the right people get to the right place at the right time. The second is to process the resulting data in such a way that the police, as managers of very expensive manpower, can give the best service to the public for a given expenditure.

The system has been used operationally since Christmas 1971. Work on applying it to management strategy has also been started. The computer is housed next to the control room, and is operated by means of a visual display unit. This is a combination of a typewriter, on which messages are tapped to the computer, and a television screen which displays them. The screen also shows information which can be obtained by the operator from the computer. There are seven visual display units in the control room and one in each of the twelve Birmingham subdivisions. Each is wired up to the computer. This is equivalent to a set of very fast teleprinters linked to the control room. The operation of the system is organised by the computer, which puts a series of set questions on the television screen. One series deals with the logging of emergency calls, a second the changing of the record of an officer's activity, a third displaying lists of men and activities, and so on. Questions and answers follow fixed sequences, which have been designed to reduce typing to a minimum. In most cases all that is required is the typing of a single number representing one of a set of standard replies.

When emergency calls are received either at the control room or subdivision, the V.D.U. operator types the relevant information into it. All he has to do is, say, type the figure '1' if it is a '999' call, or '5' if it is a fire or ambulance call. The computer then asks for, successively, the location of the incident, the name of the informant and any further details, including the subdivision. If the call comes through to the control room at headquarters, immediately the subdivision concerned is known by the computer an alert is sounded at that subdivision's V.D.U.

The Sergeant who controls it there presses a key to accept the message and receives a copy of the control room information log on his screen. The log also has on it a list of Panda cars available and a note of other men in the sub-division. In the control room at headquarters, the operator receives a list of the force cars available. Both the Sergeant in the subdivision and the control room operator can then simultaneously dispatch vehicles and log their action, again using the V.D.U. They can, of course, talk to each other over the radio if there are any queries. Other details of action can also be put into the same log by the control room and by the subdivisional Sergeant-controller.

When each car is dispatched, the computer notes the

time. If the officer reports his arrival at the scene of an incident, the Sergeant types in the code to the computer and the computer again notes the time. This is done automatically by the driver pressing a single button on a vehicle status and location device in the car.

At any time, the Sergeant can transfer the log into the computer's memory and continue with another task using the V.D.U. There are three methods of retrieving the log from the computer. Firstly, using a code, he can recall the latest incident, details of which then appear on the television screen. Secondly, if he knows its serial number, he can obtain the log for any incident. Finally, if the serial number is not known, the incident log may still be recalled using a procedure in which the computer asks for the period in which the incident occurred, the type of incident and the subdivision. The computer produces a list on the V.D.U. of all incidents which fit the specification. Clearly, if time has elapsed and the Sergeant does not know in which subdivision an incident occurred, the list is going to be much longer.

There are three displays available for recall at the control room in headquarters and four at each subdivision. The displays at the control room show respectively: a total force summary of availability, the traffic cars available, and an activity list for a specified subdivision. The Sergeant-controller in the subdivision can call up a summary of the total availability of resources in the subdivision. He can also get lists of the activities of Pandas, foot-patrols and beat officers. Each list shows the relevant call-sign, collar-number of the officer and incident or other activity. The Panda display also shows the activities of traffic cars in the division. The resource displays are designed to help the Sergeant-controller keep an up-to-date record of the deployment of the men under his control. This enables him to make routine patrol decisions more easily.

There is no doubt that the officers in the central control room at Birmingham find the system easy to handle, once they get used to tapping out the codes on the keyboard, instead of jotting down messages on to note-pads. There is a lack of tension in the room, and officers seemed to be working well within their capacities, even in handling '999' calls. Apart from the speed and ease with which information is noted and transmitted, the real benefit of the scheme is its flexibility. The Inspector in charge can take over control if an incident seems to demand it. Or action can be delegated to subdivision, if it does not. A Sergeant in one of the subdivisions handling the V.D.U. there was not so sure about its value, but nevertheless seemed to rely on it heavily, storing information via the keyboard, leaving him free to give advice to a succession of young constables coming in for instructions about their duties. The system has quite clearly demonstrated where the spine of most routine police activity is located. It is very much in the hands of the Sergeants in the subdivisions, the Sergeant and small team at headquarters under an Inspector, and especially the men on patrol. The fact that the computer stores information instead of it being transmitted on bits of paper means that in-trays in some offices are not as full as they used to be, which is making some middle-rank officers question their role.

The system will help to analyse police activity and thus manage resources more effectively. The question is whether the typical senior police officer can change his outlook overnight. The aim is, after all, to persuade him to become a manager with views on cost-effectiveness as keen as those of his equivalents in commerce and industry.

Computers will come increasingly into use as a tool of the police service. They are, for example, being used in London to aid traffic control, a scheme which began as an experiment in 1967. The computer controls traffic lights. Information from sensors in the roads about traffic flows is fed into the central traffic control room at Scotland Yard. Police can then either put in different time-plans to send traffic through or can take over control of some automatic traffic systems from the desk. Television cameras bring to screens in the control room pictures of key roads. The Department of the Environment has approved the results of the experiment, and the control room is run jointly by the Greater London Council and the Police.

The GLC has now gone into the possibility of extending it. In the west London scheme now in operation, there are 107 controlled locations: that is, seventy-four traffic lights and thirty-three pedestrian lights, covering six-and-a-quarter square miles. These were due to come under computer control in March 1973. Phase two, which is expected to come into operation by mid-1976, will extend the area to 240 square miles and incorporate 1,000 traffic lights under computer control. Each junction will ultimately have a maximum of sixteen different time plans, and 150 television cameras will enable police sitting in the control room to keep an eye on the traffic density and flow.

The economic need for investment in technology as an aid to traffic control is shown by the size of the sums involved. The police spend 10 per cent of their time on traffic duties, with an expenditure of £30 million a year. In 1972 the cost of accidents, in terms of treating people and repairing vehicles and in loss of earnings was £450 million, and the cost of congestion was estimated to be £850 million.

A variation of the application of computers to traffic problems is evidenced by a study in Sussex. Automatic vehicle sensors, buried in the road surface, are being used to measure the way in which everyday operations of the traffic police can influence driver behaviour. Computers are employed to analyse this data and show how, for example, a radar check or the presence of a marked police vehicle can be used to best effect. Computer models which re-create road accident situations are being used to discover when and where police activity will be of most benefit in reducing the number of road casualties. The work is part of a large research programme to show how the limited resources of the traffic police can best be deployed to bring about a reduction of road accidents or some alleviation of traffic congestion. If this research is successful, the benefit to the community is likely to far outweigh the sums being invested.

By far the most ambitious of the new schemes is the Police National Computer, equipment for which was installed in 1972. It is designed to provide a national bank of information about crimes and criminals based on records currently kept in manual form in the central and regional criminal records offices. The new system enables police officers on patrol, whether on foot or in cars, to get answers from the computer in a matter of minutes, through their own force communications to their headquarters and thence to Hendon, the site of the computer, by high-speed lines.

The information stored is to include details of stolen motor-vehicles, an index to the main finger-print collection, records of wanted and missing persons, and the criminal names index. There will also be a limited amount of information to enable the police to make inquiries about the owners of vehicles and, at a later stage, centralised records of disqualified drivers and persons subject to suspended sentences.

The system is required to work for twenty-four hours a day on every day of the year and, to meet this need during periods of routine maintenance and breakdown, most of the central equipment is duplicated. During the initial stages of use, developed during 1974, there are about 100 teleprinter and 200 visual display unit terminals in police force headquarters all over the country connected to the computer. By 1980 it is planned to have between 800 and 1,000 terminals on line to the computer centre.

Since the nineteenth century, central records of all 'major' criminals – people who have committed indictable offences – have been kept in London. But between the wars the London criminal record office began to be overloaded and offices were opened in Preston and Wakefield to cater for the North of England. These, too, began to be congested, with the result that forces found a slower response to their inquiries. So a series of regional records offices grew up in places like Bristol, Manchester and Durham, in order to enable forces to receive a quick response to information about local crime. There were ten such centres by the 1960s. In addition, Forces kept their own records and the CID also had information it thought worth preserving. This meant that, when a policeman needed to have comprehensive information about people, he would have to send out widespread requests, hoping that something would turn up from one of the offices. The problem was further complicated by the increasing pressure, as well, on Scotland Yard, as a result of the increase in crime.

The Police National Computer is intended not only to store a properly classified, complete list of information centrally, but to provide data at very high speed to the ordinary policeman on the beat, as well as to the CID man in his office. If a policeman on the beat becomes suspicious about a car or person, he can get information, via his headquarters, from the Police National Computer in time to apprehend the suspect, if justified. The limited amount of information being fed into the computer about car-owners will include names. If the police want to check the name of the owner of a car, that will quickly be forthcoming. The special index of stolen vehicles will likewise enable policemen to obtain rapid responses to inquiries.

An index to the national finger-print collection will also be on the machine. The system is intended to save widespread manual searching, often involving many hundreds of prints. Instead, a much smaller number is thrown out by the computer as the most likely to compare with the prints the officer has, with resultant considerable savings in processing time. Missing and wanted persons will be listed. The Police National Computer will also, at a later stage, contain some information at present published in the *Police Gazette*, such as 'a left-handed criminal with a club foot who breaks in on Saturday nights', and an index to stolen property and cheques will be included.

The Home Office has created a training scheme for between 1,000 and 1,500 police and civilian staff for their preparation as terminal operators for the first phase of operations, and more operators will be trained as later stages of the project develop.

All the terminals through which the computer can be contacted are in secure rooms in police offices, with special precautions to limit access only to authorised personnel. Those who do have it must use certain call signs in what is known as a 'hand-shake routine'. Each terminal has its own key which the computer recognises, like a safe combination. This also works as a minute-by-minute log of transactions, so that, if anyone is in any doubt afterwards, he can check when the call was made and by whom. Nothing is being kept on the computer that is not already filed in manual form.

The computer will help policemen to reach decisions about arrests, by providing information about suspects with a record. Its speedy availability will also tighten checks at entry and exit points to the country, for instance against the shipment of stolen cars or criminals making a getaway.

Though the Home Office is providing the computer for the police, it is not for government use. It is for police use. As it is of constitutional importance that police and government remain separate, pains have been taken to ensure that the availability of information is properly regulated, and the number of people able to put in requests for it to the computer directly is strictly limited. A log of transactions will be available to each Chief Constable as required in order to check that details needed have been received. From 1974, the Police National Computer is costing between £2½ million and £3 million a year to run, and this cost is shared between the government and local authorities.

The way in which science may be able to save police

time and money is shown by research, still incomplete, at the Home Office Scientific Group at St Albans, into methods of locating buried bodies. The need for improved techniques was indicated by the Moors murders, but it is, unfortunately, a recurring one. A few years ago in Cannock Chase some small girls went missing. Then a nine-year-old girl was seen accepting a lift in a car and being driven away. That was reported to the police at 6 p.m. on a Saturday. By 10 a.m. next day a search force of 9,000 had been mobilised. They had to divide up the search area and crawl through heath, heather and woods, trying to discover traces of her. Eventually she was discovered in a shallow grave, murdered. The skeleton of another child was under the soil nearby.

At St Albans graves have been dug experimentally, some filled with pig carcases and others left with nothing in them. An attempt was made using a specialised type of photography to picture the extent of chlorophyl in the plants, which gives off infra-red reflection. It is possible, by this means, to see where the chlorophyl is deficient. The presence of a body in a grave at first reduces the chlorophyl – the grass fades – but then it recovers, and grows with extra vigour. One weakness of the method is that other things can make grass fade – for example, a cow lying on it. Another method tested is the use of thermal cameras to try and detect where the soil has been disturbed and the absorption of heat is different. A third method is to pound the soil, and, by use of seismic equipment, plot vibrations through it, which charts the presence of objects below.

The war against crime is producing ideas as imaginative as those thrown up in 1939–45. Top scientists advising the Home Office pointed out that certain creatures had built-in sensors which enabled them to detect carcases. Trying to discover what they are has led to a fascinating line of inquiry.

A series of dog trials was run scientifically. The first set was designed to show what the probability was of different

breeds of dogs being able to find the bodies. Areas of sixteen metres by sixteen metres were split up into four-
metre squares distributed through woods and sandy soil.
Whole pigs were buried or the graves filled up with nothing in them. The time and depth of burial were varied.
One alsatian and one border collie were taken over the
areas in turn, to each of the four-metre squares. The dogs
had to decide whether or not there was a pig there. The
dog handler did not know. The results showed that the
training of dogs for this purpose paid off. A second set of
trials was designed to simulate a real search and covered
a larger area. Seventeen areas were in fact chosen, each
covering between two and five acres of all sorts of vegeta-
tion and soil. Out of the seventeen trials, thirteen were
successfully concluded. A total of eight burials were discovered and five areas declared to be free of pigs. Most of
the areas were searched in two hours or less. The conclusion was that dogs can be trained successfully to look for
bodies, and could thus help to reduce the numbers of men
needed in a search. The need is now to discover the most
suitable breed, and advice on this has been sought from
the Royal Veterinary College.

The ability of foxes to discover buried remains has also
been examined. There was hearsay evidence that they were
good at it. The laboratory at St Albans got hold of some
foxes but they were not amenable to training, so fox cubs
were tried. They were kept from each other and the most
suitable, 'Fred', was chosen. A girl was employed to look
after him. Fred also underwent familiarisation training
with men. Meat was put round the site, and Fred was asked
to look for it. Fred behaved well in some people's company, but on the whole was not very good at working with
humans. Although Fred had a keener nose than a dog, he
would not cover the ground as thoroughly.

The phoridae fly was also tried. Dead pigs were buried
in a field and a trap set for the flies, which were then
hand-counted. A map was drawn indicating where the
concentration of flies was heaviest. The phoridae flies

had clustered where the graves were. In an attempt to use flies as a detector, some of them were grown from larvae and carried over the ground in a box to see whether, by their excited buzz, it was possible to find the graves. Another experiment tested whether it was possible, by using sensitive equipment, to pick up the noise of the flies' wing-beats remotely.

When this failed – the flies were of no use in winter anyway – scientists went for advice to the British Museum, which recommended use of the sexton beetle. It is said that this will go for many miles to find a carcass in which to lay its eggs. Using a dead mouse as bait, scientists trapped some of the beetles. Again it was not possible to detect remotely the noise they make, when excited, by rubbing their back legs together.

It is in the field of crime detection that science has been longest established. Sherlock Holmes's analysis of cigar ash has long seemed elementary. One of the latest developments is a new technique which will enable detectives at the scene of a crime to photograph footprints and other impressions on, say, carpets that would previously have been totally invisible. The technique, called holographic interferometry, uses a characteristic of most composite or fibrous materials – such as wood, plastics and woven materials – to creep very gradually back into shape after being deformed by a stealthy footprint.

Light from a ruby laser is shone on an area where the presence of impressions is suspected. Reflected light from the area and direct light from the laser beam are combined on a photographic plate to form a hologram. Then, five minutes or so later, another hologram is exposed on the same photographic plate. Any minute differences in the reflected light, due to movements in the area under examination, show up on the double exposure of the hologram. The result looks a bit like a contour map. The technique is being refined to a point where it may soon be available for use by police forces.

The use of science by police forces has been on a

formally organised basis for over thirty years in England and Wales, since the setting up of the Metropolitan Police laboratory and Home Office regional laboratories. The Home Office Central Research Establishment, established in 1966, has the function of exploring new techniques and equipment, and of investigating new areas of science which may be exploited for the benefit of crime investigation.

There are regional Home Office laboratories, the cost of which is shared by the local authorities and government, at Nottingham, Harrogate, Newcastle, Chorley, Birmingham, Cardiff, Bristol and Aldermaston. All together, there are now over 400 scientists doing police work. One Home Office laboratory specialises in the examination of firearms and another in the examination of questioned documents.

One of the main roles of the Central Research Establishment is the dissemination of the latest scientific knowledge for easy reference. Each year its scientists read about 350,000 titles on subjects ranging from paint to explosives and from glass to poisons. About 2,500 papers a year go on file, and relevant ones are sent monthly to the regional laboratories. Microfilms are produced annually of all material stored. A computer-based retrieval system, especially tailored for forensic science, is in the final stages of development. Video-tapes are made for the training of police officers, so that they know what to send to the laboratories.

The increase in crimes of violence means that police 'scenes-of-crime' officers are sending to the laboratories more and more exhibits of blood, semen, hair and other biological materials. The suspect may be connected with the victim of an assault by a few small blood-stains on his jacket. New methods of analysing blood are revealing the extent of differences between individuals. Before long it may be possible to single out individuals by means of their blood as is done now by the use of finger-prints. Existing techniques of blood-grouping and enzyme measurement may make it worthwhile to take blood or saliva from every one in a small community in an effort to pick out the few individuals who, from their genetic make-up, fall within the suspect group. The same sort of method may be of use in tracing the writer of an anonymous letter by means of the saliva left when the envelope was licked and sealed.

Latest techniques of analysing metal are already achieving convictions. In one case a sawn-off shotgun was left at the scene of a crime and a hack-saw was found in a suspect's house. The tiny particles of metal on the hack-saw matched that of the shotgun. Research has enabled tiny fragments of paint and glass, found on a suspect's clothing, perhaps after breaking in to commit murder, to be used as evidence. Previously, a sliver of glass, made in large scale production, was thought to have no value as evidence. Now even day-to-day variations between glass from the same furnace can be detected. After a hit-and-run killing, it is now possible to say whether a fragment of glass found on the body came from the lamp of a suspect's vehicle.

Tiny flakes of paint on a man's clothing can also send him to prison. If there are several layers of paint in the flake, the value of the evidence can equal that of a fingerprint.

The way that these scientific discoveries and painstaking police work were used to trace the assailant of a seventeen-year-old Sunday school teacher is a classic example of modern detection at its best. Her body was discovered on 3 January 1972, partly concealed behind a hawthorn hedge at the end of a track leading into some fields at Bryning Lane, Wrea Green, near Kirkham, Lancashire. Only one of her shoes was found there. The cause of death was given by Dr B. Beeson, a Home Office pathologist, as asphyxia due to pressure on the neck. There were also scratches on the body, which could have been caused by barbed wire or the hawthorn hedge.

Clues found at the scene were analysed and the results given to the police on the assumption that one or more of them were connected with the vehicle in which the girl was carried to where she was found. It was deduced that the most likely type of vehicle would be a pre-1964 BMC type of the Austin A60 size – although no car was manufactured with the particular combination of colours or materials, of which traces had been found. This suggested that the car had been resprayed and could contain certain parts from other vehicles.

Many samples of car paint, car seat upholstery, car carpets and tyres were sent, as the result of diligent police work, to the laboratory for comparison. One set of samples was taken from a 1960 MG Magnette, which police found in a scrap yard at Poulton-le-Fylde, near Blackpool. The Magnette's body had been painted over black on top of red and the number plates had been painted over black. It had blue leather seats and dark red carpets. The tyres were not still on the vehicle, but three of the four were recovered.

The clues from the girl's clothing (fibres, leather and paint) all matched the samples from the car in composition and fine detail. Tyre tracks from the field corresponded, even down to the mark of a repair plug, with the tyres found. One of the carpets had an eight-and-a-half inches long head hair on it like the victim's.

Extensive police inquiries showed that the car had been bought in October 1971 by a man and taken to the scrap yard by a friend of his on or about 16 January 1972. The previous owner had painted the car with two different colours of red paint and had some carpets from an Austin A60 transferred to it. The original colour of the car had been light blue with grey carpets.

A saliva sample from the suspect showed that he was a blood group B secretor, which tallied with traces found at the scene. He was charged with the girl's murder on 28 April 1972, nearly four months after the body was discovered. Found guilty of manslaughter, he was sentenced to ten years' imprisonment. At the trial he admitted being with the girl in the car when she died, but maintained that this had happened when he put his hands on her throat to quieten her. The detectives were in the Lancashire

Force and the scientists at the Home Office Forensic Laboratory at Chorley.

The examples quoted in this chapter give some indication of the extent of the scientific revolution facing the police. The question is, what effect will it have on the nature of policing and of the police themselves?

Conclusion

*Science and the future police role – how governments
have failed the police – bureaucracy a danger to liberty –
why the police are over-defensive – suggestions for reform.*

In which direction are the police going? In ten years'
time it will be 1984. The kind of police we have then will
depend very much upon the policies being created now.
So far there has not been the fundamental reappraisal of
the role of the police that is now needed in order to take
into account the far-reaching changes that are facing them.
The title of this book, *The Police Revolution*, does not,
of course, imply that anarchy is about to reign within the
police service. It reflects the impact of changes, including
science and technology, which, whether the police like it
or not, will raise questions both about the traditional ways
in which they work and their relationships with the public.
The changes are external as well as internal.

This book has attempted to show that much for which
the police are blamed has causes that lie beyond their
control. If, for political reasons, there is a gap between
government and people, the task of the police in maintaining public tranquillity is made more difficult. If children
become violent and commit vandalism after being reared
like battery hens in tall blocks of flats, and the crime rate
goes up, people wonder why the police cannot prevent it,
and instead more youths are stopped in the street for
behaving suspiciously. If traffic suddenly jams in a city
centre and no policeman instantly appears to sort it out,
his absence is criticised and contrasted with the alacrity
with which his colleagues run-in speeding motorists and
give breathalyser tests. And if international fraudsmen
thumb their noses from abroad at powerless detectives, the
victims cannot have a very high opinion of law enforcement.

Home Secretaries, of course, defend the police against criticism. Without their dedication, society would fall apart. But, in defending the police, there is a reluctance on the part of Home Secretaries to acknowledge that some of the criticism may be valid, not necessarily because of shortcomings on the part of the police, but because they have been put in an impossible position by the failure of governments to take action that could relieve the pressure on them. The attitude of successive governments has been not unlike that of certain Generals in the First World War. If the political strategy is wrong and public turbulence results, it is the policemen in the front line who wipe the spittle from their faces, link arms and nurse bruises. Because policemen do not enter into politics, their voice remains unheard. This silence is sometimes misunderstood by some protesting groups with which they have to deal. The police are accused of being repressive and are said to enjoy being so. Ask any young policeman if he enjoys giving up his weekends to face demonstrators, and he will say he does not. He would prefer to be at home with his long-suffering wife, who thinks he is never there when he is needed. The young policeman goes home, perhaps, to more misunderstandings after spending an afternoon already under pressure from a demonstration. To rely on the police to keep down the lid of the pressure cooker when the gas should be turned down, exposes them to the danger of being scalded. It is little wonder that policemen who say that they are doing their best feel a sense of grievance at the criticism they receive from sectors of the public. Yet the police, attempting to meet some of it, are, happily, prepared to accept some change in the complaints procedure, though some people concerned about civil liberty feel that they are reluctant to go as far as they should.

Governments have, in fact, taken advantage of the sense of duty of the British police service by not doing enough to reduce the points of stress. Moreover, the way in which boundary changes have been introduced to police force areas has been reprehensively high-handed and without proper regard for the ordinary policeman. If a mob burned down Parliament, no doubt M.P.s would blame the police for not preventing it. It is only because of the police that government ministers can mouth platitudes that they 'will not be coerced'. Maybe not. But when the government stands firm in the politics of confrontation and people protest, it is the police who act as a buffer. In this sense, the police are being used as the government's force. If the government, as in the Macmillan era, is concerned with consensus, the task of the police is made easier. Consensus politics mean that the police can be regarded as truly 'our' police. If Prime Ministers are abrasive, it is the police who suffer the abrasions.

This does not, of course, mean that Britain is on the verge of becoming a police state. It is more in danger of becoming a bureaucratic one. Most policemen genuinely believe that they are upholders of liberty: the liberty to protest, the liberty of people to feel safe in their beds at night, the liberty to drive on roads without too great a fear of being killed because the police are there to breathalyse those who constitute a danger and to prosecute the road-hogs.

The real danger lies, not with the police, but with the bureaucrats, who operate anonymously in a government which has become too remote, locally and nationally, in ever bigger units within which the size of the disaffected minorities must increase. In bigger governmental units it becomes increasingly difficult to please all the people all the time.

It is not that the police are themselves blameless, but before seeing what the police have to do to put their own house in order, it is necessary to see what they are to blame for. In this respect the controversy over the use of the Special Patrol Group is worth further examination. It was created partly to deal with problems that arise because officers cannot easily cope with certain situations on the spot. If there were enough men in London to patrol the streets as they should be patrolled, with sufficient knowledge of people in the area they serve for police to be able to exercise adequate discretion, the presence of the Special Patrol Group would not be necessary. No one can quarrel with certain other of the tasks set the Group, such as dragging ponds for missing youngsters, or setting up road blocks to catch gun-men. This is a valuable public service. But a decision to use the Group on some other duties requires sensitive judgement and careful briefing of its officers.

The short-sighted failure of governments to take adequate steps towards the proper policing of London has left the Metropolitan Police, in particular, facing a grave manpower crisis, and other Forces are also suffering shortages. Not only is preventive policing made more difficult, but the pressure on the police means that they cannot give the attention to all crime in the way they would like. Moreover, the shortage of men increases pressure on individual policemen. It is when policemen are tired, overburdened, and cannot be given the supervision everyone would like, that any tendency on an individual's part to cut corners is increased. The police are extended beyond the call of duty, and it is time that this was remedied by the government.

In the face of criticism directed against them for reasons which lie beyond their control, the police are apt to react over-defensively. Whitewash is sometimes applied too indiscriminately. They sometimes assume the worst of their critics, refusing to acknowledge the honesty of candour, and a few policemen would wish to discredit them. In fact, the police are sensitive to criticism, but are slightly baffled sometimes to know what they can do about it. There is a danger that they then retreat into their Victorian bastion, as one policeman put it, and isolate themselves within it. There are already pressures towards the isolation of the police. Shortage of manpower is one of them. Another reason is that policemen are expected to have high moral standards while the rest of the world is permissive. In fact, strange as it may seem to some of their critics, the police are human. They err. But a distinction has to be drawn between errors that are human and those which arise from the worst sin a policeman can commit – deliberate misuse of the power with which the public entrusts him on its behalf, whether for personal gain, for some mistaken idea that the ends of justice are being better served that way, or as a frustrated and angry response to provocation.

Many of the Victorian ideals on which the police were founded still hold good today, even if, because of modern pressures, some of them seem to lie beyond attainment. Victorian ideals often were unattainable, even to Victorians, and this led to their common vice of hypocrisy. But the best of these ideals were within reach. They emphasised the impartiality of the police in dealing with all sections of the public, whatever their race. They emphasised the qualities of compassion and courtesy. They emphasised a sense of duty. They emphasised the need for upholding the law with an understanding sense of discretion.

This book cannot provide a charter of all the measures needed as the result of a reappraisal of the police. But any analysis ought to be constructive. The first need is to give the police proper political priority, not merely in the provision of sufficient pay to attract enough recruits of the right calibre, but in the introduction of measures that will reduce external pressures. The police need to be consulted more when planning decisions are made, to help create crime-free estates and accident-free road systems. They ought, indeed, to be involved when committees sit on even such with-it subjects as pop-festivals. Lincolnshire Police, for example, know a lot about the way they are run. The police have tremendous practical knowledge and experience which could be of more use to the community and which is not being adequately employed. Somehow the tendency towards isolation and defensiveness has to be reduced. Home beat schemes of sufficiently small size and the reversal of the trend away from traditional village policing are two ways in which this could be achieved. The local police station, with its fund of knowledge, needs to be regarded more as a social agency nerve centre, and the prejudice of some welfare workers against the police must be reduced. They have much to offer each other. The police need to be integrated more into local government at a level that matters. In London this implies a closer alliance between the Metropolitan Police and the boroughs in which they operate, with perhaps more autonomy being given to the divisional commander.

Such bodies as the National Association for the Care and Resettlement of Offenders are awakening to the realisation that merely to look after people when they have offended is not enough. Prevention of crime is important too. An obvious common interest here provides opportunity for more police involvement. The Scottish system of having one police branch to deal with both crime prevention and community liaison deserves to be copied.

The police are introducing methods of screening to ensure that they do not get too authoritarian-minded recruits. There are already mind-broadening courses for policemen. These are to be welcomed. Their weakness is that they tend to be available mainly for policemen who, for career reasons, realise that their minds need to be broadened. Nevertheless, they will find it difficult to lead the more narrow-minded constables and sergeants, in whose hands lies much of the day-to-day running of the police service, and certainly the formation of police attitudes. It is a good sign that seminars on local problems are being held in Metropolitan Police stations. There is a case for temporarily detaching narrow-minded sergeants and constables in their early thirties to some form of work that will broaden their outlook and experience and prevent prejudice. There are courses already in which policemen are taught simple facts about immigrants. These need to be extended. Perhaps more study ought also to be given to the tribalistic rites, customs and attitudes of the police service. 'Know thyself', is a motto policemen might appreciate. As we have seen, their situation and characteristics may have more in common with black people than either side realises. Those black people who work in police canteens and elsewhere seem to get on well with them. The trouble is that sociologists on the whole find it difficult to talk a language that policemen can understand. Professor Michael Banton, of the University of Bristol, is a glowing exception and has done as much as possible to bridge this gap.

At the Police College, Bramshill, and other training centres, more attention ought to be given to the training necessary for the technological age of policing. In particular, the full implications of the revolution facing the police ought to be studied. Policemen have a natural and healthy scepticism towards technology. If some of them do think of the cost of computers in terms of boot equivalents, this may be because the boot is just as important. Without a comfortable pair of boots, the policeman cannot happily pound the beat, and if he cannot pound the beat, he loses contact with the public. And if his feet are wet and he has corns, the contact he does have may well be painful.

Technology is no substitute for human police officers, and the technologists realise this. Indeed, insensitively used, technology can increase the gap with the public that the police are so concerned to bridge. Properly used, however, with adequate safeguards to prevent abuse, technology can be an invaluable tool of modern policing. Indeed, it is essential. The policeman's natural scepticism about technology reflects that of the general public, who do not easily trust what they cannot easily understand.

The computer system being developed in Birmingham could, if used properly, contribute towards greater and more helpful contact between public and police. If it reduces the amount of paper-work, more men can be freed for work with the public instead of with each other. A complaint frequently heard among constables is that there are more chiefs than Indians in the police service. Better and more organised information could reduce the time needed to reach decisions, and fewer chiefs may then be needed to ponder them.

If the technology is insensitively used, more exacting control of individual officers could reduce the opportunity for them to take decisions themselves. The worst effect could be to remove responsibility from the individual officer's shoulders to such an extent that he finds difficulty in exercising it. This would give the police a regimented unity and central control alien to this country. The police are made up of individual human beings each making decisions and exercising discretion. This provides a most valuable system of checks and balances and gives policing a human face, provided the individuals are motivated correctly.

It is steady, reassuring contact with friendly policemen that people want, with policemen who are in touch with local knowledge, who understand them and can act on their own initiative when that is needed. They want policemen to be a source of ever-present help in time of trouble. The police service is unlike some other manpower-intensive industries developed in Victorian times. In the police service technology cannot be a substitute for people. The service has to remain manpower-intensive. And this will cost money and demand political will.

A new definition of the role of the police could be: to save people from the worst that they can do to themselves, to each other and to the government. The weakness of this definition is that the police cannot, because they are non-political and must remain so, save the people from the worst that the government can do to them. That is up to the government and Parliament and the health of the democratic system. There is time, before 1984, for the government and the more prejudiced critics of the police to become aware of that.

Bibliography

Thieves on Wheels by David Powis (a *Police Review* publication, 1971).

Social Trends No. 3, 'Crimes of Violence against the Person in England and Wales' by Stanley Klein, edited by Muriel Nissel, Central Statistical Office (HMSO, 1972).

Firearms' Control by Colin Greenwood (Routledge & Kegan Paul, 1972).

A Man Apart by Anthony Judge (Arthur Barker, 1972).

The Police in Society (the Police Federation, 1971).

Society and the Policeman's Role by Maureen Cain (Routledge & Kegan Paul, 1973).

Scotland Yard by John Deane Potter (Burke Books, 1951).

Police State by Brian Chapman (Pall Mall, 1970).

This Little Band of Prophets by Anne Fremantle (The New American Library, 1960).

The Police by Ben Whitaker (Eyre & Spottiswoode, 1964).

Destroy this Temple by Obi Egbuna (MacGibbon & Kee, 1971).

'Aetiology of Traffic Accidents' by A. B. Clayton and G. M. Mackay, *Health Bulletin*, Vol. 31, No. 4, pp. 277–80 (October 1972).

The Criminologist, 'Public Attitudes to the Police' by Monica Shaw and W. Williamson, Vol. 7, No. 26 (Autumn, 1972).

Attitudes of Young Immigrants by Peter Evans (Runnymede Trust, 1971).

Hansard, Col. 849 (17 November 1969, HMSO).

Police Power and Black People by Derek Humphry (Panther Books, 1972).

Select Committee on Race Relations and Immigration (evidence) (29 March 1973, HMSO).

The Police We Deserve, J. C. Alderson and Philip John Stead (eds.) (Wolfe, 1973).

Murder Investigation by Frederick Oughton (Elek, 1971).

Europe Tomorrow by Richard Mayne (Fontana, 1972).

Future Shock by Alvin Toffler (Bodley Head, 1970).

Defensible Space by Oscar Newman (The Architectural Press, 1973).

Criminal Organisation by Donald R. Cressey (Heinemann Education, 1972).

Index

www.ingramcontent.com/pod-product-compliance
Ingram Content Group UK Ltd.
Pitfield, Milton Keynes, MK11 3LW, UK
UKHW031301020325
455728UK00026B/524